Fit to Paddle

Fit to Paddle

The Paddler's Guide to Strength and Conditioning

 Ragged Mountain Press / McGraw-Hill

 Camden, Maine • New York • Chicago • San Francisco
New Delhi • San Juan • Seoul • Singapore • Sydney

ROCKY SNYDER, C.S.C.S.

Certified Strength and Conditioning Specialist

- Lisbon • London • Madrid • Mexico City • Milan •
- Toronto

The McGraw·Hill Companies

1 2 3 4 5 6 7 8 9 10 DOCDOC 0 9 8 7 6 5 4 3

Library of Congress Cataloging-in-Publication Data
Snyder, Rocky.
  Fit to paddle : the conditioning guide for kayakers and canoeists / Rocky Snyder ; forewords by Dave "The Wave" Johnston, Eli Helbert.– 1st paperback ed.
      p.   cm.
Includes bibliographical references and index.
  ISBN 0-07-141952-7
  1. Canoes and canoeing—Training. 2. Kayaking—Training.
3. Exercise. I. Title.
  GV783.S56 2003
  796.1´22—dc21   2003007436

Questions regarding the content of this book should be addressed to
>   Ragged Mountain Press
>   P.O. Box 220
>   Camden, ME 04843
>   www.raggedmountainpress.com

Questions regarding the ordering of this book should be addressed to
>   The McGraw-Hill Companies
>   Customer Service Department
>   P.O. Box 547
>   Blacklick, OH 43004
>   Retail customers: 1-800-262-4729
>   Bookstores: 1-800-722-4726

Title page photo by Brian Bailey/Imagestate. Photo on pages 9 and 11 by Howard "Boots" McGhee (bootsite.net). All other photos by Scott Lechner. Illustrations on pages 76, 77, and 165 by George Arentz.

To Dad.
The best paddling partner I ever had.
May you rest in peace.

Contents

Foreword by Eli Helbert 8

Foreword by Dave "The Wave" Johnston 10

Preface 12

Acknowledgments 14

Introduction 15

Chapter 1   Creating Your Program 17

Chapter 2   Flexibility Training 22

Chapter 3   Sun Salutation 59

Chapter 4   Endurance Training 72

Chapter 5   Strength Training 83

Chapter 6   Medicine Ball Training 118

Chapter 7   Stability Ball Training 128

Chapter 8   Sample Workout Programs 139

Appendix 1   Exercises at a Glance 159

Appendix 2   Workout Log 162

Appendix 3   Resources 164

Appendix 4   Muscle Chart 165

Index 166

Foreword

by **Eli Helbert** *Two-Time World Champion of Open-Canoe Rodeo*

As a veteran of competitive open-canoe rodeo and creek racing, I've spent countless hours training to maintain my body at a peak performance level. I have worked at keeping my muscles strong while maintaining flexibility, in order to hold off the challenges presented by other competitors.

Like Rocky Snyder, I was introduced to canoeing through the Boy Scouts. On my path to the rank of Eagle, I learned to set high goals for myself that I could achieve with a visual plan. After I graduated from college, I followed the same formula to achieve my goal of becoming a world-champion canoeist.

As a paddling instructor, I'm always on the lookout for useful texts to recommend to my students. Rocky's *Fit to Paddle* lays out structured progressions to build endurance, power, and flexibility in a format specific to paddling. *Fit to Paddle* offers recreational paddlers a program for keeping their body in shape, within a practical amount of training time. At the same time, the book is a valuable resource for experienced paddlers seeking better exercises, for camp counselors looking for fun drills and activities, or for anyone who simply wants to condition their body and stay active.

My own training consists of spending as much time on the water as possible. I add to this several yoga poses, and I try to stretch whenever I have a free moment. I typically prefer pull-ups, crunches, and push-ups to traditional gym exercises, due to my traveling lifestyle. I also use a stability ball in my training program to incorporate added body balance into the strength I maintain.

In *Fit to Paddle*, Rocky gives step-by-step details on a wide range of excellent exercises so you can build just the personalized training regimen that works best for you. These are activities to ensure your solid conditioning for paddling. In most cases, they can be performed wherever and whenever you choose.

A modest amount of time and effort expended on the program you develop with the help of *Fit to Paddle* can reward you with significant

improvements in your paddling and in your energy level. As your endurance, strength, and flexibility increase, your paddling strokes and movements will be more powerful and you will experience more fun and success.

I look forward to seeing you on the water with a smile on your face. Good luck!

Foreword

by Dave Johnston World Champion of Surf Kayaking, 2001, 2002, 2003

There is nothing like the feeling of shoving off in a kayak. When all the preparations are done, all the logistics are complete, and you finally float upon the water, it's as if the weight of the world has been lifted from you. Suddenly you are suspended on a new medium where the rough edges of gravity have been softened. The sport of paddling has magical powers that can beautifully change lives. Once you are hooked, you want to enjoy it as often and for as long as possible.

You may be someone who loves to glide over glassy flatwater while watching for wildlife and nature. Or you may yearn for the adrenaline rush of whitewater. Or you may paddle the sea. Whether you go via the safety of a harbor or by blasting through the surf, you will be using your own type of craft and your own set of muscle groups. Paddle sports are varied, and so are the training routines you have to choose from.

While some injuries from paddling are common, active training can help with both prevention and cure. Injuries have many causes, such as poor paddling posture, improper boat fit or lifting, or the over-working of tight muscles. A good fitness program can shorten your recovery time or help you to avoid injury in the first place.

You need to create your own training balance to help you perform better and avoid injury. After nearly twenty years of teaching, guiding, and competing, I believe that cross-training, using a variety of activities in addition to your time in kayak or canoe, is the key to developing the balance needed to enjoy year after year of paddling fun.

This yin and yang of paddling has many aspects. Two of the most important are strength and flexibility. Most beginning paddlers are lacking in one or both of these. Strength training, including paddling and sprints, plus arm and shoulder exercises, can sharpen the learning curve for beginners. More flexibility means you can stay out longer, and it also reduces the chance of injury. Forward bends and other yoga postures stretch out your hamstrings and reduce tension in your lower back.

Whitewater and surf paddlers need strength and flexibility to perform repeated Eskimo rolls in conditions that may have severe penalty clauses attached for failure. Side stretches, forward bends, and back bends for flexibility, and crunches, and back extensions for strength, are easy to do with an exercise ball.

Advanced and competitive boaters need rigorous cross-training activities to balance rigorous paddling—for example, running or biking followed by swimming. To win, you need strength and flexibility, but also a balance of endurance and power. That is what Rocky Snyder's *Fit to Paddle* is all about. This book offer details on programs of stretching and strengthening and endurance that you can use to create a personal training routine for taking you to the next level of paddling pleasure and achievement.

You can't always go out on the water when you want to, but you can help ensure many more opportunities in the future by staying fit to paddle.

Preface

I was eleven years old when I first sat in a canoe. Boy Scout Troop 705 was spending a weekend on the Saco River in Maine. My dad, determined to share in my childhood adventures, became my canoeing partner. Little did I realize that this canoe would be the vehicle in which my father and I would truly discover each other. We talked about friendship, broken hearts, and our first romantic crush; about the Boston Celtics and the New England Patriots; and about what it really means to be a man.

The sandy-bottom Saco River crept along for miles, but to me it felt like we were flying. As we paddled downstream, troop leaders instructed us on paddling techniques, water safety, and how to read the river. On the second day we encountered our first and only set of rapids. It was a fifty-foot stretch of class 2 whitewater—but to this boy it was the rapids of the Snake River! After that weekend I was addicted to the exciting world of whitewater canoeing. My father got us a fifteen-foot orange canoe and we used it every chance we got.

Over the next few years, Dad and I tackled some of the fiercest rivers in New England. Rivers with tongue-twisting names like the Pemigawasett, Androscoggin, Contoocook, and Penobscot were the places where we honed our whitewater skills. In early spring, as soon as the ice broke off the river's edge, we were on the water. During the summer we took extended voyages on the rivers that rush through the Canadian and Northern Maine wilderness. When autumn set in we prayed for rain to bring water levels back up before ice once again formed on the banks. In the bitter winters of New England we discovered, to our delight, what an excellent sled the canoe made. Unfortunately, steering left much to be desired and we resembled an orange bobsled of destruction careening through the forest.

I was fourteen years old when my dad bought a new toy: a kayak! Naturally, I was at the stage where I was trying to gain some semblance of personal independence. Perhaps Dad knew this and that's why he got the kayak. I think he used it only a few times before I considered it mine.

By today's standards that kayak turned like an aircraft carrier on a sea of maple syrup, but back then it was lightning on water. Sadly, one day we awoke to find that someone had stolen it from our backyard. I sure do miss that kayak, but I am grateful that its loss got the two of us back together in the canoe for one more year. My dad's health started to diminish and our days as a team would soon come to an end. Perhaps because of this eventual loss of my canoe partner due to my dad's illness, I then became a fan of whitewater rafting. Throughout my college years, I took friends rafting down the rivers of western Massachusetts and southern Vermont.

After college I moved to Santa Cruz, California, where I was hired at a local health club and began my career as a personal fitness trainer, becoming certified as a strength and conditioning specialist (C.S.C.S.). This combination of paddling experiences and fitness training skills eventually led me to write *Fit to Paddle*.

For me the thrill of tackling whitewater has transformed into a passion for surfing, but I still maintain a strong connection to my first love. I participate in outrigger canoe races, often tour Monterey Bay in an ocean kayak, and go on excursions to the rushing rivers of the Sierra Nevada Mountains.

Whenever I reminisce on all my times spent on the water in all sorts of craft, the moments I cherish most are those when the river was calm and a father and his son could learn about each other in a beat-up old orange canoe.

Acknowledgments

The idea for this book would not have found ink and paper had it not been for my friends and family who continued to encourage me. Thanks go out to Ramona d'Viola for her patience during photo shoots. I would also like to express my thanks to Frank Stockwell, the shining leader of Boy Scout Troop 705 in Reading, Massachusetts, when I was a boy. Without his hard, selfless work, I and many others would never have shared in the countless adventures we experienced through the backcountry of New England and Canada many years ago.

Introduction

People of all ages are discovering the freedom and fun they can have
on the water. But in today's world of timesaving and laborsaving devices, many people have become less active on a day-to-day basis. This
sedentary existence combined with infrequent bouts of activity can
lead to what has been called the weekend-warrior syndrome—caused
when a person experiences injury because he or she plays too hard
on the weekends, following a work week that involves little physical
activity. Common injury sites for paddlers are the neck, shoulders, elbows, and lower back. Paddlers need a conditioning program that increases strength, endurance, and flexibility while reducing the risk of
injury.

Articles in canoeing or kayaking magazines sometimes feature an
exercise or stretch for the water enthusiast. Yet there is little information on complete conditioning programs for any paddle sport. This
guidebook will not tell you where to find the best rivers and lakes,
how to paddle, how to shoot the rapids, or any of the other basics of
rafting, canoeing, or kayaking. What this book will do is give you the
tools needed to be better conditioned for the activities you so enjoy.

I have been a personal fitness trainer in Santa Cruz, California, since
1992. I've trained a number of competitive and recreational kayakers,
rafters, canoeists, and outrigger canoeists. When asked why they chose
to train with me, these athletes said the primary reason was that the
conditioning programs I designed were specific to their sport.

Sport-specific training is an area in which many health clubs fall
short. When someone joins a commercial gym, this new member usually works out an exercise program with the help of a staff member.
The typical program is a general conditioning routine designed for
overall fitness—a program that resembles a bodybuilder's workout.
Unless there are medical concerns, most exercise programs will be
almost identical. These generic programs are not necessarily bad, but
they could be better designed to meet the specific goals of the
individual.

Fit to Paddle offers a comprehensive, sport-specific approach to conditioning. It is designed to fight the weekend-warrior syndrome in a safe and effective manner. The programs can be adapted for use by anyone, regardless of gender, age, or fitness level. You do not have to be a member of a health club for this approach to be effective. Many of the exercises can be performed at home or on the water.

The chapters of this book provide information on creating a personalized conditioning routine; they describe exercises that contribute to strength, endurance and flexibility; and they give sample conditioning programs for both gym and home and for during camping trips.

Before getting started, here are a few rules to follow:

- Before beginning any new exercise program, it is strongly recommended that you consult your primary health-care provider.

- Execute proper form during all exercises and stretches. If the form is incorrect, different muscles must compensate—and the more compensation that occurs, the higher the potential for injury.

- If you experience dizziness, discomfort, or pain, stop immediately.

- The final rule: have fun!

Chapter 1

Creating Your Program

In creating your own conditioning program, start out slowly. Progress to more intense workouts only as your body gets accustomed to these exercises.

People who have exercised regularly in the past but have not exercised vigorously for several months, or even years, sometimes try to start a new exercise program where the old one left off. This can be dangerous because their muscles have deconditioned—even though their egos have remained intact. The chance of injury or extreme muscle soreness is greatly increased. It's important to start out slowly so the body can adapt to the new strains that exercise places on the body.

If any sharp pain is experienced while performing an exercise, stop immediately. The exercise may not be the right one for you. Check the description in this book of the exercise to see if you were performing it correctly. If it was performed properly, yet you still felt pain, omit that exercise from your conditioning program.

Following are some tips to help you develop an overall conditioning program that combines three cornerstones of physical conditioning: flexibility training, endurance training, and strength training. All three types of training will then be discussed and illustrated in detail in the chapters that follow.

Flexibility Training

Flexibility is the key to injury prevention. Strength training and endurance programs have a tendency to tighten the muscles, so it's essential to stretch the body back to a balanced state.

Stretching exercises are used as warm-up for strength and endurance training. Most gains in flexibility, however, come when stretches are performed after such training. Be sure to take time at the end of each workout to properly cool down via stretching. The flexibility portion of your fitness program should be carried out as often as possible, however, even if the other parts of the program are not performed as frequently.

Endurance Training

Endurance training includes such activities as swimming, running, and various forms of paddling. By alternating these various cardiovascular exercises, your body is challenged to meet many different types of movement. This can help reduce the chance of experiencing a plateau in training in which your body no longer develops at the desirable rate you've been experiencing.

In designing the endurance (cardiovascular) portion of your program, start slowly and progress to higher intensity in a methodical manner. Start with 10 to 20 minutes, two or three times per week, and add 5 to 10 minutes each week or add an additional day.

Many people gauge the intensity of their cardiovascular routine by their heart rate, using a target heart rate to monitor whether they are exercising at an ideal intensity level. Generally speaking, when you exercise at 60 percent of your theoretical maximum heart rate or above, desired physiological adaptations occur. Exercising at 100 percent of your maximum is not recommended. A range of 65 to 85 percent of the maximum heart rate is a safe range for most people. Anyone with medical concerns should consult a physician before establishing a desired heart rate for cardiovascular exercise.

To determine a target exercise heart rate, you can use a very simple equation, although the only factor taken into account is your age. Subtract your age from 220. The resulting number represents your theoretical maximum heart rate. Multiply that maximum heart rate by the desired exercise percentage (intensity) that you select (most likely between 65 and 85 percent) to find your target heart rate. For example, the theoretical maximum heart rate for a 40-year-old paddler would be 180; multiplying by a desired percentage of, say, 70 percent would result in a target exercise heart rate of 126. This is the simplest way to determine a target heart rate.

A better equation, the Karvonen Method, takes both a person's resting heart rate and age into consideration in determining the target heart rate. The best time to take your resting heart rate is in the morning, before getting out of bed. Count your pulse for 1 minute. This is your resting heart rate. The equation is as follows:

Maximum Heart Rate (220 – Age) – Resting Heart Rate x Desired Percent + Resting Heart Rate = Target Exercise Heart Rate

For example, a 50-year-old woman with a resting heart rate of 63 beats per minute wishes to exercise at an intensity of 75 percent of her maximum heart rate.

220 – 50 (age) = 170 (maximum heart rate)
170 – 63 (resting heart rate) = 107
107 x 0.75 (desired percent) = 80
80 + 63 (resting heart rate) = 143 (her target heart rate)

Use of a measurement known as the rate of perceived exertion (RPE) is a more subjective way to determine your desired intensity level. Simply put, on a scale from 1 to 10 (1 being very easy and 10 being maximal effort), how intensely do you think you are exercising? To determine your own personal target zone, warm up and then build to a submaximal yet challenged effort after a few minutes of endurance activity, such as paddling or running. Your heart rate at that point will be your target heart rate and will be between 5 to 8 on your RPE scale. Ideally a person should exercise between 5 and 8 on that scale.

Using both the Karvonen formula and the rate of perceived exertion may be a wise course of action. A combination of both approaches can provide a more accurate estimate of the correct intensity level for your endurance training.

Strength Training

Strength training consists of relatively short bursts of muscular force anywhere between 1 second and 2 minutes. This type of training helps build size and strength in the muscles and conditions them to store more energy for immediate use. One to two days per week of strength training is considered a maintenance routine with little change in strength levels. Three days or more brings about physiological changes. Strength training sessions may vary between 10 minutes and two hours or more depending on the training protocol. I generally recommend 30 minutes to one hour, three to five days per week, to experience the physiological benefits of this kind of training.

- When performing strength training exercises, start by executing one to two sets of each exercise selected.

- After exercising for a week, you can increase the sets from two to four per session.

- With most strength training exercises, perform between 8 and 15 repetitions in a set.

- If you cannot do an exercise with proper form for 8 repetitions, chances are the weight is too heavy.

- If you can do an exercise with proper form for more than 15 repetitions, the weight is probably too light.

- For exercises that do not incorporate the external resistance of weights (such as dumbbells or barbells), you can magnify the intensity by increasing the repetitions. Among these non-weighted exercises are abdominal and lower back exercises, push-ups, and pull-ups. Each set can include 10 to 30 repetitions.

It's a good idea to change your list of exercises on a regular basis so that muscles do not get too accustomed to the same movement. The greater variety you add to a strength workout, the greater the different number of demands you place upon the muscles—with the advantage that it forces them to adapt in a number of ways. Try changing the list of exercises each week or every other week. It's OK to repeat some of the same exercises, but be sure to alternate at least two or three of them.

Workout Programs

Chapter 8 provides detailed workout programs that are samples of the ones you can choose for your own fitness routine, including exercises for flexibility, endurance, and strength. One program is a 10-week plan for use at a gym or health club; one is a 10-week program that encompasses the same conditioning goals but can be carried out at home; and one is a program for overnight camping excursions.

Chapter 2

Flexibility Training

The wind and waves are always on the side of the ablest navigators.

Edward Gibbon

One of the most important elements in fitness, yet often the most overlooked, is flexibility. When muscles have more tension than they should, an imbalance is created and the body's movement is restricted. This makes any activity require more effort.

It is through lengthening (stretching) tense muscles and tightening (strengthening) weak muscles that the body is restored to a balanced state. The more balanced the body, the more efficient its movements—and the less likely that an injury will occur. The following pages contain photos and descriptions of stretching exercises that help to create a better balance of tension and contribute to flexibility.

Stretching exercises are often referred to as poses, because the stretch puts you into a pose that you will hold for a period of time. Holding a pose for 10 seconds is good, but 30 seconds to a minute allows more time for muscles to balance. Performing the stretch more than once can also bring better results.

If any stretch causes pain, stop immediately and omit it from your program for the time being. As your body achieves a higher degree of balance, certain stretches that previously caused pain can often be performed without pain. Every body is different. Therefore, not all poses are effective for everyone.

The following stretches, or poses, are grouped into four categories:

lying, kneeling, sitting, and standing. When creating your own flexibility program, choose a few stretches from each category in order to benefit a full range of muscles.

The photos and descriptions in this chapter are designed to get you familiar with the stretches and to serve as a reference once you've started your training routine. Chapter 8 provides detailed workout programs that incorporate these various stretches.

Lying Stretches

Elbow Presses

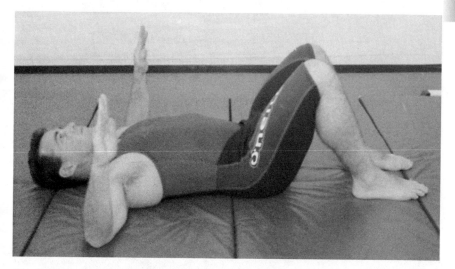

1. Lie on your back with knees bent and feet flat.

2. Place your arms perpendicular to your body and bend your elbows so the fingers point to the ceiling.

3. Press your elbows into the floor for 1 second, then relax.

4. Your shoulder blades should slide together, then apart.

5. Perform at least 2 sets of 10 to 30 repetitions.

Benefit: Promotes shoulder stabilization.

Pullovers

1. Lie on your back with knees bent and feet flat.

2. Clasp your hands together, with fingers interlocked.

3. Straighten both arms above the chest and shoulders. [1]

4. Lower your arms over your head to the floor, or as far as possible without pain. [2]

5. Keep your lower back in contact with the floor.

6. Bring your arms back to the starting position.

7. Perform at least 2 sets of 10 to 30 repetitions.

Benefit: Reduces tension in neck and upper back.

Crossed Knee Lift

1. Lie on the floor face up, with your arms straight out from the sides of your body and palms down.

2. Cross one ankle over the opposite knee.

3. Lift the knee up directly above the hip and hold for at least 15 seconds.

4. Repeat using the opposite leg.

5. Hold for 15 seconds to 1 minute.

Benefit: Promotes proper muscular balance in hips and back.

Crossover Twist

1. Lie on the floor face up, with your arms straight out from the sides of your body and palms down.

2. Bend the knees at right angles so your feet are flat on the floor.

3. Cross one ankle over the opposite knee.

4. Keeping shoulders and arms on the floor, rotate the leg and the crossed foot over to the side until both rest on the floor.

5. The knee that is not on the floor should point up to the ceiling.

6. Hold for 10 seconds to 1 minute.

7. Repeat using the opposite leg and foot.

Benefit: Promotes proper muscular balance of hips and lower back.

Hamstring Stretch with Strap

1. Lie on the floor face up, with a non-elastic strap wrapped around the arch of the foot.

2. Hold the ends of the strap in each hand.

3. Lift the straight leg up in the direction of the shoulder.

4. When a stretch can be felt in the hamstring, apply gentle tension to the strap by pulling with your arms.

5. Hold each stretch for at least 2 seconds.

6. Perform 5 to 10 repetitions before changing legs.

Benefit: Reduces knee, hip, and lower back tension.

Calf Stretch with Strap

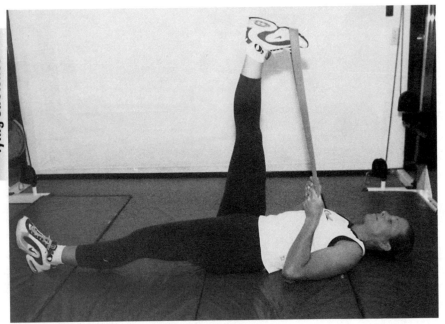

1. Lie on the floor face up, with a strap wrapped around the ball of one foot.

2. Hold the ends of the strap in each hand.

3. Begin the stretch with the straight leg above the hip.

4. Point the foot to the ceiling, then flex the foot downward toward your head.

5. When a stretch can be felt, apply gentle tension to the strap by pulling with your arms.

6. Hold each stretch for at least 2 seconds.

7. Perform 5 to 10 repetitions before changing legs.

Benefit: Reduces ankle and knee tension.

Superhero

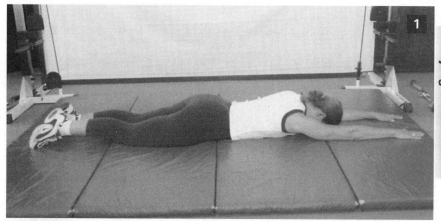

1. Lie face down, with your arms in front of your body. [1]

2. Exhale as you gently lift your upper body off the floor. [2]

3. Inhale as you return your body to the starting position.

4. Keep your toes in contact with the floor at all times.

5. Perform at least 2 sets of 5 to 10 repetitions.

Benefit: Helps strengthen mid and lower back.

Crocodile Twist

1. Lie on the floor face up, with legs straight.

2. Bring your arms straight out from the sides of your body, with palms down.

3. Place your left heel on the toes of your right foot. [1]

4. Keep both legs straight as you rotate both feet and legs to the right, as close to the floor as possible. [2]

5. Hold for at least 10 seconds.

6. Switch legs and rotate to the right.

Benefit: Promotes proper spinal rotation.

I.T. Band (Iliotibial Band) Stretch with Strap

1. Lie on the floor face up, with a strap wrapped around one arch.

2. Hold both ends of the strap in the opposite hand.

3. Lift the straight leg up in the direction of the opposite shoulder (toward the hand holding the strap).

4. When a stretch can be felt, apply gentle tension to the strap by pulling with your arm.

5. Hold each stretch for at least 2 seconds.

6. Perform 5 to 10 repetitions before changing legs.

Benefit: Reduces knee, outer hip, and thigh tension.

Upper Spinal Floor Twist

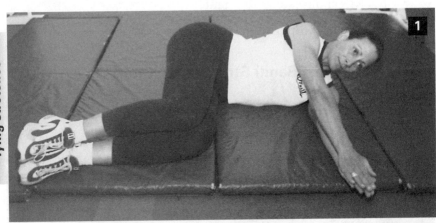

1. Lie on one side, with your knees pulled up into right angles with your hips and ankles.

2. Extend your arms in front of your body, with palms together. [1]

3. Exhale as you reach over your body with the upper arm and down to the floor on the opposite side. [2]

4. Keep your legs firmly anchored to the floor so the rotation occurs in the spine and torso.

5. Hold for 10 seconds to 1 minute.

6. Repeat on the opposite side.

Benefit: Promotes proper spinal rotation and torso flexibility.

Upward-facing Dog

1. Begin in a push-up position, with arms and legs supporting your straight body above the floor.

2. Inhale as you bend your arms and lower your body toward the floor—but don't touch the floor.

3. Exhale as your chest pulls forward and upward and your arms press into a straightened position.

4. Perform at least 2 sets of 2 to 10 repetitions.

Benefit: Promotes spinal flexibility and upper body strength.

Kneeling Stretches

Mad Cat Stretch

1. Support your body on all fours, with your hands below the shoulders and your knees below the hips. [1]

2. Breathe out as you arch your back upward. [2]

3. Breathe in as you bow your back downward.

4. Move your head in the opposite direction of the back.

5. The movement should be continuous, without pausing at the top or the bottom.

Benefit: Promotes better movement in the back, shoulders, and hips.

Crossed Arm Stretch

1. With elbows bent, cross one arm above the other so one elbow is nestled in the pit of the opposite arm.

2. With the hand of the lower arm, grasp the opposite wrist, with both arms pointing upward.

3. Pull both elbows downward and hold for at least 15 seconds.

4. Switch arms and perform the same stretch.

Benefit: Stretches neck and shoulder muscles that tighten during paddling.

Note: This exercise can be performed kneeling or standing.

Arm Circles

1. Extend your arms out from the sides of your body at shoulder height.

2. Keep your shoulder blades pinched together as your arms make 6-inch circles backward, with palms face up. [1]

3. Flip your palms down and reverse the circle direction. [2]

4. Keep your body as still as possible, with movement occurring only at the shoulder joint.

Benefit: Promotes ball and socket movement in the shoulder for proper paddling technique.

Note: This exercise can be performed kneeling or standing.

Downward-Facing Dog

1. Begin on your hands and knees so the hands are directly below the shoulders and the knees are below the hips.

2. Push your body up and back so it is supported on the hands and feet.

3. Press your hips back so the spine lengthens and straightens.

4. Maintain the spinal position as both arms and legs lengthen, but without the elbows or knees hyper-extending, or "locking out."

5. Hold this pose for at least 2 sets of 10 seconds to 3 minutes.

Benefit: Reduces lower back tension by stretching the hamstrings and calves while strengthening the shoulders and midback region.

Modified Shoulder Stand

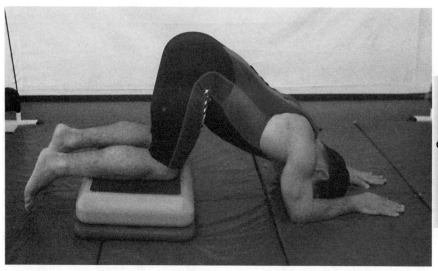

1. Kneel on a flat surface 3 to 10 inches above floor level. The higher the surface, the more intense the exercise.

2. Place both elbows and forearms on the floor, palms down, so your shoulders are below the hips.

3. Your hips should be slightly forward of the knees.

4. Your forearms should be parallel, with the elbows directly below the shoulder joints.

5. Lower the crown of your head as far to the floor as possible.

6. Allow your body's weight to sink so your shoulder blades fall together.

7. Hold still in this pose for 15 seconds to 2 minutes.

Benefit: Reduces lower back and neck compression; strengthens muscles responsible for proper posture.

Shoulder Pivots

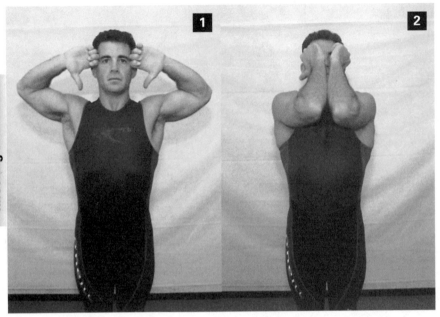

1. Place the knuckles of your index and middle fingers against the temples of your head.

2. Face your palms forward, with the thumbs below the fingers. [1]

3. Exhale as you pull your elbows forward until they touch. [2]

4. Inhale as you pull your elbows back as far as possible.

5. The knuckles should act like hinges on a door; do not lift them off the temples.

6. Perform 1 to 3 sets of 10 to 30 repetitions.

Benefit: Promotes proper shoulder joint movement and strengthens the rotator cuff muscles.

Note: This exercise can be performed kneeling, seated, or standing.

Side Lateral Raise

1. Place your arms directly by the side of your body, with palms in. [1]

2. Exhale as you lift your straight arms sideways to shoulder height.

3. Flip your palms toward the ceiling and raise your arms above your head until the palms contact each other. [2]

4. Reverse directions and rotate your hands down at shoulder height.

5. Keep the rest of your body as motionless as possible during the exercise.

6. Perform 1 to 3 sets of 5 to 30 repetitions.

Benefit: Promotes proper shoulder joint movement and reduces shoulder rotation.

Note: This exercise can be performed kneeling, seated, or standing.

Sitting Stretches

The Frog

sitting stretches

1. Sit upright as tall as possible.

2. Bend at the knees to bring the soles of your feet together.

3. Gently press the soles together so your knees lower closer to the floor.

4. You can place your hands upon the knees to gently assist in pressing your legs toward the floor.

5. Continue to sit as tall as possible during the pose.

6. Hold for 10 seconds to 1 minute.

Benefit: Stretches inner thigh muscles and helps strengthen proper sitting muscles.

Boat Pose

1. Sit on the floor with both legs together and straight in front of your body.

2. Lift both legs off the floor as you lean your torso slightly back.

3. Extend your arms forward, just outside of your legs.

4. Keep your torso firm and back straight so your body forms a right angle at the hip joint.

5. The balancing point will occur at the sit bones (the lower portion of the pelvis), located at the base of the buttocks.

6. Hold for 10 seconds to 1 minute.

Benefit: Strengthens thighs, hips, and abdominal muscles while promoting balance.

Sitting Floor

1. Sit with your hips, back, shoulders, and head against a wall.

2. Extend both legs in front of your body, with your feet pointing straight to the ceiling.

3. Keep legs 3 to 4 inches apart.

4. Maintain a constant contraction in the quadriceps muscles (top of the thigh).

5. Sit as tall as possible during the pose.

6. Hold for 10 seconds to 1 minute.

Benefit: Stretches hamstring muscles and promotes strength in the proper sitting muscles.

Modified Hurdler Stretch

1. Extend the right leg in front of your body, with the foot pointing straight to the ceiling.

2. Bend the left knee to bring the sole of the foot against the inner thigh of your right leg.

3. Bend at the hips as you lean your torso forward in the direction of the right leg. If possible hold the foot or ankle with one hand.

4. Be sure not to bend through the spine instead of the hips.

5. Hold for 10 seconds to 1 minute before switching legs.

Benefit: Stretches one hamstring at a time to create a bilateral balance of tension.

Seated Torso Twist

sitting stretches

1. Sit in a chair, with your knees parallel and at right angles to the hips and ankles. Your feet should point straight ahead.

2. Remain in a tall seated posture as you twist your torso to the right as you reach around to the top of the backrest with your right hand.

3. Hold on to the bottom-right corner of the seat with your left hand.

4. Keep hips and legs facing forward so the rotation occurs in the spine and torso.

5. Hold for 10 seconds to 1 minute before switching sides.

Benefit: Improves torso and lower back flexibility.
Note: This stretch can be performed while seated in a boat.

Simple Twist

1. In a seated position, bring your right leg behind your body by bending at the right knee.

2. Place the sole of your left foot against the top of your right knee and thigh.

3. Remain in a tall seated position as you reach back behind your body with your left hand and twist your torso to the left.

4. Keep your left hand anchored to the floor and bring your right hand to the left knee to assist in the twisting.

5. Hold for 10 seconds to 1 minute before switching sides.

Benefit: Improves flexibility of the spine, waist, and front side of the hip.

Seated Lower-back Stretch

1. In a tall seated posture, straighten your right leg in front of your body, with the foot pointing to the ceiling.

2. Bend at the left knee and cross the left foot over the right leg and down to the floor so that the foot can be pulled flat toward your groin.

3. Place your left elbow against the inside of your left knee as you reach around with your right arm and then anchor it to the floor behind your body.

4. Hold for 10 seconds to 1 minute before switching sides.

Benefit: Improves flexibility to each side of the lower back.

Note: For a variation of this stretch, carry out the exercise without crossing one leg over the other, or twist in the opposite direction.

Standing Stretches

Bar Hang

1. Use a pull-up bar or other sturdy object from which to hang.

2. Grab the bar outside of shoulder-width.

3. Gently relax your shoulders as your body sinks toward the ground.

4. Hold for 10 seconds to 1 minute.

Benefit: Reduces spinal compression, stretches shoulders and back, and improves grip strength.

Chest and Shoulder Stretch

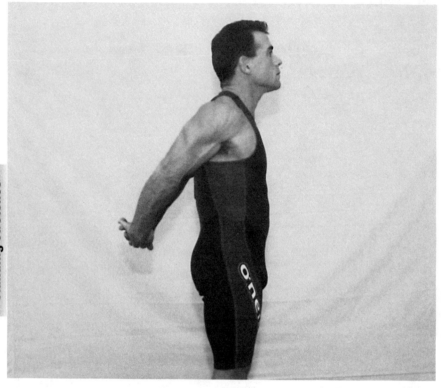

1. Stand with your feet parallel and knees slightly bent.

2. Clasp both hands together, with fingers interlocked behind your back.

3. Straighten both arms and push your hands away from your body.

4. Keep your body upright, making sure your torso does not bend forward.

Benefit: Stretches chest and shoulder muscles that tighten when paddling.

Warrior Pose

1. Stand with your legs 3 feet apart.

2. Keep your right foot pointing forward and turn your left foot sideways so your feet are perpendicular to each other.

3. Extend your arms out from the sides of your body at shoulder height.

4. Bend your left knee while your right leg remains straight as you shift your body's weight sideways to the left. Turn your head to the left.

5. Hold for 10 seconds to 1 minute before switching sides.

Benefit: Stretches inner thigh and strengthens leg and core muscles.

Triangle Pose

1. Stand with your legs 3 feet apart.

2. Keep the right foot pointing forward and turn the left foot sideways so your feet are perpendicular to each other.

3. Extend your arms out from the sides of your body at shoulder height. [1]

4. Bend your hip and waist to the left so the left hand contacts the lower portion of your left leg.

5. Turn your head toward the ceiling. [2]

6. Hold for 10 seconds to 1 minute before switching sides.

Benefit: Stretches and strengthens muscles at the hips and waist.

Side Reach

1. Stand with your legs 3 feet apart.

2. Keep the right foot pointing forward and turn the left foot sideways so your feet are perpendicular to each other.

3. Extend your arms out from the sides of your body at shoulder height.

4. Bend your left knee while your right leg remains straight as you shift your body's weight sideways to the left.

5. Lower your left hand to contact the left ankle as you reach up and over your head with your right arm.

6. Hold for 10 seconds to 1 minute before switching sides.

Benefit: Stretches torso muscles while strengthening leg muscles.

Reverse Triangle Pose

1. Stand with your legs 3 feet apart.

2. Keep the right foot pointing forward and turn the left foot sideways so your feet are perpendicular to each other.

3. Extend your arms out from the sides of your body at shoulder height.

4. Bend and rotate at the hip and waist to the left so your right hand contacts the lower portion of your left leg.

5. Turn your head toward the ceiling.

6. Hold for 10 seconds to 1 minute before switching sides.

Benefit: Stretches and strengthens muscles at the hips, waist, and lower back.

Wall Sit

1. Get into a sitting position against a wall so your lower back is flat and your knees and hips are the same height from the floor—as if sitting in a chair.

2. Your feet should be 4 inches apart, pointing straight ahead and parallel.

3. Your feet should be away from the wall so the heels are directly below the knees.

4. Ankles, knees, and hips should all be at right angles.

5. The weight of your body should be pressed through the heels and not the toes.

6. Hold for about 30 seconds.

Benefit: Enhances leg strength and proper posture and reduces lower back tension.

Wrist Stretch

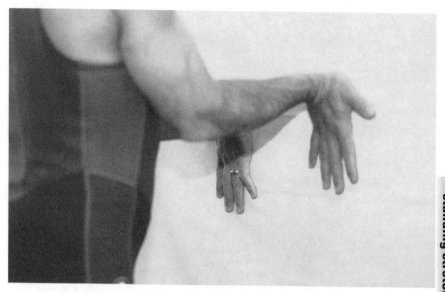

1. Stand 4 inches away from a wall, with your feet parallel and one shoe-width apart.

2. Place your palms against the wall, with fingers pointing to the floor.

3. The hands should be at a height that allows the elbows to be at right angles and nestled into the side of the body.

4. Keep your shoulders lowered as both shoulder blades are pulled together.

5. Hold for 10 seconds to 1 minute.

Benefit: Stretches forearm muscles that tighten when paddling; strengthens midback muscles while stretching the chest muscles.

Advanced Shoulder Stretch

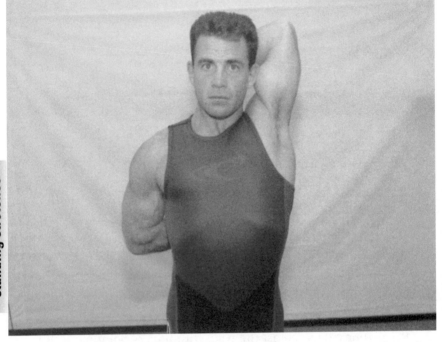

1. Bring your right hand behind your back so the fingers reach up between the shoulder blades.

2. Bring your left hand behind your head and neck so the fingers point down toward the opposite hand.

3. Bring both hands together so the fingers grip one another.

4. Hold for 10 seconds to 1 minute before switching sides.

Benefit: Stretches shoulder muscles and increases range of movement.

Note: You can grip a paddle or a towel with both hands if you're not able to get your hands close enough together for grasping fingers. This exercise can be performed standing, seated, or kneeling.

Chapter 3

Sun Salutation

Watch your habits, for they will become your character. Develop your character, for it becomes your destiny.

Anonymous

The Sun Salutation is a series of gentle, flowing yoga poses that are often performed as a morning wake-up routine. The Sun Salutation can also be performed as a warm-up routine prior to paddling. This series of movements enhances flexibility of the spine and legs and chest while strengthening the arms and shoulders and enhancing the body's sense of balance and coordination.

Try to hold each pose for 5 to 15 seconds before transitioning to the next pose in the sequence. Perform the series of 12 poses three to four times. When performing the repetition of the lunge position, be sure to alternate legs. A single sequence of the 12 poses usually takes about one minute.

Concentrate to maintain an awareness of your breath while entering and exiting each pose. When breathing, be sure to inhale into the diaphragm, filling the midsection as deeply as possible.

Prayer Pose

1. Stand tall with your feet at hip width.

2. Gently press your palms together in a prayer position.

3. Inhale deeply.

Mountain Pose

1. Exhale as you reach upward with both arms.

Forward Bend

1. Inhale as you bend your body forward.

2. Lower your torso, with arms reaching forward.

3. Bring your hands to the floor as the back bends slightly.

Lunge Position

1. Bend both knees, with hands flat on the floor.

2. Exhale as you step back with your right foot until the left knee is at a right angle.

3. Allow your midsection to rest against the top of your left thigh.

Plank Position

1. Bring your left leg back parallel to the right leg.

2. Inhale as you keep your arms straight to support the body's weight.

3. Keep torso and legs straight so the body resembles a plank.

Grasshopper Pose

1. From the plank position, bend at the elbows and knees.
2. Exhale as you allow your body to lower until your chest almost scrapes the floor.

Upward-Facing Dog

1. Inhale as you press your chest upward and forward as your arms and legs straighten.

2. Keep the thigh muscles contracted to help support your body.

Downward-Facing Dog

1. Exhale as you push your body backward onto your hands and feet as the legs, arms, and back straighten.

2. Press your heels to the floor while maintaining straight legs and push the hips away from the hands.

3. Point the sit bones at the base of the buttocks toward the ceiling.

Lunge Position

1. Bend both knees, with hands flat on the floor.

2. Inhale as you step forward with the right foot until the right knee is at a right angle.

3. Allow the midsection to rest against the top of the right thigh.

Deep Forward Bend

yoga warm-up

1. Bring your left foot forward to be parallel with the right foot.

2. Exhale as you bend your body forward.

3. Inhale as you raise your torso, with arms parallel with the spine.

Mountain Pose

1. Exhale as you reach upward with both arms.

Prayer Pose

1. Stand tall with feet together as you lower your arms.

2. Gently press your palms together in a prayer position.

3. Inhale deeply.

4. Repeat entire sequence of poses.

Chapter 4

Endurance Training

Just keep going. Everybody gets better if they keep at it.

Ted Williams

A paddler requires not only flexibility and strength for heavy paddling but also muscular endurance to maintain stamina for an entire session. In creating an effective endurance program of cardiovascular activities, four elements are critical.

Increasing or upgrading any one of these elements will increase the demands placed on your body as it works to develop the cardiovascular fitness essential to endurance.

These elements are:

- Frequency: The number of times the endurance exercise is performed in a particular period of time.

- Duration: The length of time it takes to perform the exercise.

- Intensity: The effort level reached during the exercise.

- Type: The choice of exercise performed in a workout.

This chapter concentrates on cardiovascular exercises that are either specific to paddling (such as resistance paddling, interval paddling, and paddle relays) or can serve as cross-training activities (such as swimming, stair climbing, running, and bicycling).

It's helpful at this point to understand the *overload principle*—the general idea that by overloading or exhausting muscles in a careful, systematic manner, physiological changes will occur that make the muscles stronger and more durable. A person paddling for the first time quickly becomes exhausted. But with a program of progressively tougher workouts, that individual should grow stronger as his or her muscles are taxed to a higher and higher point of fatigue. This principle will come into play as you develop a program of increasingly rigorous endurance activities.

The photos and descriptions that follow will familiarize you with various endurance drills and exercises. You can refer back to them as you progress in your personal training program. See chapter 8 for detailed programs that include these exercises and offer recommendations on duration and intensity of the workouts.

Paddling Activities to Build Endurance

It may seem obvious, but to become a stronger paddler, you need to paddle. A basketball player shoots baskets. A marathon runner runs. And a paddler incorporates a good bit of paddling into a well-rounded fitness program.

There are many endurance drills for paddlers. Regardless of which ones you choose, be sure to maintain proper posture and form while paddling. Improper form forces the body to compensate, placing stress in new areas and increasing the chance of injury.

You can go ahead with some of the following exercises on your own, while others involve more than one boat. Rally the troops for a workout on the water: the drills can be a good deal of hard work, but they're also a lot of fun.

Resistance Paddling

Get a plastic bucket with a sturdy handle, or use a large coffee can. Drill holes in the container until it looks like Swiss cheese. Tie a length of rope to the container so it can be attached to the stern of your kayak or canoe. Paddle this way for just half the time of your normal paddling session, building up slowly until you are able to paddle this way for the length of an entire paddling session.

The bucket adds tremendous resistance as you paddle. The fewer holes you drill, the more resistance you'll feel as you work to paddle against the dead weight of the water-filled bucket.

Paddling Upstream

Runners perform a drill called hill repeats. The runner sprints up a long hill and walks back down, then sprints back up again. This drill is repeated for several sets.

You can carry out the same type of drill on a river. Find a swift stretch of water and paddle upstream for a distance of 50 to 200 yards. At that point, turn around and slowly paddle downstream to the starting point.

Back at the beginning, paddle upstream again. Repeat this drill for 5 to 10 sets.

Interval Paddling

Interval paddling mixes short, fast stretches of paddling with intervening recovery breaks. Warm up by paddling at a comfortable pace for at least five minutes. After the warm-up is complete, break into a fast, hard sprint. After a predetermined time or distance is covered, revert back to the comfortable paddling pace until you feel recovered or until your pulse drops below your target exercise heart rate (see the section on endurance training in chapter 1).

Repeat this speed-up and slowdown 5 to 15 times. A good distance for these high-intensity intervals is between 50 and 100 yards. If you decide instead to paddle for a set amount of time, a good choice is between 15 seconds and 1 minute.

Partner Towing

With a paddling friend, take turns pulling each other's kayak or canoe with a towline, an activity guaranteed to build endurance. You can count the number of strokes and then switch leads when you reach a particular number. You might also choose to change positions after an interval time of 1 to 5 minutes or a distance of 50 to 200 yards.

Drafting Paddle

Most moving objects create a draft, pulling energy toward the back of the object from behind. The field of energy behind the object allows the objects following the first to use less effort while maintaining the same velocity. Bike racers and runners often using drafting as a technique to allow those in the back a bit of a rest. In this drill the technique is applied to paddlers. This drill involves three or more boats and usually a distance of somewhere between 500 and 1,000 yards. To start, you might do well to select a shorter distance, increasing it as you and the other participants gain conditioning.

Have the boats line up one behind the other in a straight line. The lead paddler starts out fast, with the rest close behind. The last boat in line has to break away from the line and overtake the leader. As soon as this last boat takes the lead position, the boat that is now last in line must battle to take over the lead. Some people might remember this as "Indian sprints" when conditioning for such sports as soccer, running, and football.

Continue the drill until the desired distance is covered or until every boat has been in the lead.

Tug-of-War

With two boats facing in opposite directions (see illustration, page 76), connect a rope to the stern of each. Tie a handkerchief midway along the rope. Position two flotation devices about 10 feet apart—each 5 feet from the handkerchief.

Now comes the fun: blow a whistle to begin the tug-of-war. When one of the paddlers pulls the other far enough that the handkerchief reaches a flotation device, the battle is over.

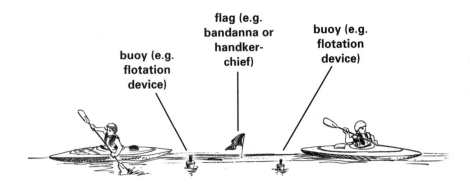

buoy (e.g. flotation device)

flag (e.g. bandanna or handkerchief)

buoy (e.g. flotation device)

Back-Paddling

Paddling backward incorporates many of the opposing muscle groups of forward paddling. So much time is spent training the forward paddling movements that the opposite muscles get neglected.

A body that develops a balance of muscle tension becomes very efficient. Therefore, try back-paddling as an endurance routine.

Paddle Relays

Start with a minimum of eight boats and divide the group into two teams. Half the boats in Team A and half the boats in Team B remain at the starting line, while the rest of the boats get in position at a turnaround point 50 to 100 yards away.

As the whistle blows to start the relay, one paddler from Team A and one from Team B paddle their boats furiously to reach and tag a teammate at the turnaround. Once tagged, a paddler races as hard as possible back to the starting line to tag another compatriot, who then takes off. Continue the relay until the last boat finishes.

For added incentive, have the winning squad choose a fitting punishment for the losing team. Make the losers load boats and gear back on the trailer, or let them buy dinner for all.

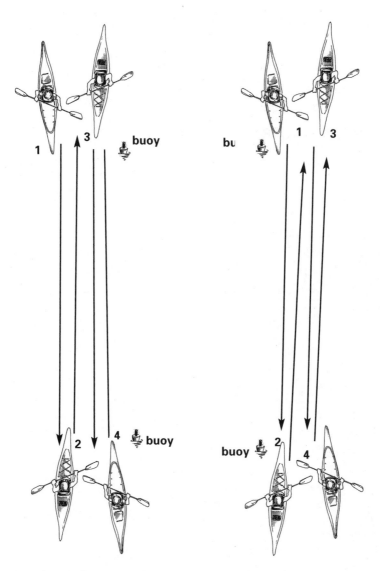

Note: this drill can also be performed with four boats. Instead of the straight sprint shown, boats would sprint to the buoy, turn around, and sprint back to the start where they tag their teammates, who then start. This can be repeated as often as desired.

Other Activities to Build Endurance

There are plenty of ways to build endurance for paddle sports in addition to paddling itself. Among them are a variety of cross-training drills—activities that are distinct from paddling on the water but are important to fitness and conditioning, such as swimming and running.

Land Paddle with Resistance Bands

During the dead of winter or when the weather turns nasty, but you still want a paddle workout, you can make use of a rubber resistance band (preferably one with handles). They're available at sporting goods stores.

Secure the middle of the band to an immovable object (such as a table leg) a few feet off the ground. Hold on to both ends of the resistance band, kneel or sit on a flat padded bench, and mimic the motions of paddling (see photos opposite). The farther the bench is placed away from the band's point of attachment, the more resistance you'll be working against. Check for wear in the band and replace it if you find any tear or abrasion; you don't want it to break, snapping back at you.

Resistance bands can be purchased at sporting goods stores.

Rowing Machine

Indoor rowing machines such as those used at commercial gyms provide a great full-body workout and a terrific cross-training exercise. Be sure to maintain good seated posture at all times. Use the legs as much as possible, because they have the body's biggest muscles. Exhale when

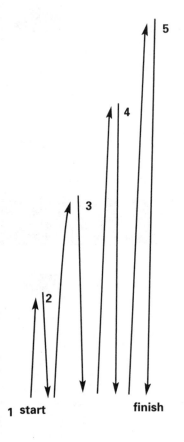

5

4

3

2

1 start   **finish**

pulling the handle inward. Some rowing machines even accept attachments that convert the device into a kayak or canoe simulator.

Suicide Drills

Set up five solid markers on the beach in a straight, evenly spaced row that totals about 40 yards. These five markers can be most anything: rocks, water bottles, pieces of driftwood—even lines in the sand. Sprint from the first marker to the second and back to the first. Then sprint to the third marker and back to the first without stopping. Then to the fourth marker and back to the first. Then finally to the fifth marker and back. Allow 2 minutes of recovery time before beginning the next set. Perform 3 to 4 sets.

You can carry out the same drill while paddling on the water, using flotation devices spaced 10 to 20 yards apart.

Water Sprints

In knee-high water, sprint on foot for 20 to 40 yards. Allow 1 to 2 minutes of recovery time before beginning the next set. Be sure the running surface is level and free of rocks and reef for safety reasons. A pool is the best place. This drill can also be done on soft sand or set up as a relay to keep things interesting.

Walking and Running

Whether you walk or run doesn't really matter: you'll reach the same destination eventually. It just might take more time if you walk. They are both good choices as part of an endurance training routine.

Whichever you choose, stand as tall as possible. Keep your head over your shoulders; chest up, and hips tucked under. Let the arms swing freely forward and backward, and keep your feet pointing straight ahead. Start with 20 minutes and build from there. (Refer to the sample programs in chapter 8 for additional recommended times.)

Stair Climbing

Cross-training with stair-climbing machines at health clubs can provide a good workout. But if there is a long flight of stairs in your neighborhood—preferably of wood rather than unforgiving concrete—try going up and down these for an endurance workout.

When climbing stairs, maintain the same form as in running or walking: stand tall. Walk slowly on the way down to allow your body and heart rate to recover. (Refer to the sample programs in chapter 8 for recommended times.)

Drafting Runs and Cycling

If you run or cycle in a group, the same technique described earlier in this chapter for the Drafting Paddle drill can be used. Form a straight line and take off. The last person must overtake the leader. Continue this process of catch-the-leader until the desired time or distance is reached, or until everyone has been in the lead.

For safety reasons choose a route with little or no traffic. It may be a good idea to run or cycle on a track or run in a park or forest.

Swimming

Swimming is great cross-training exercise—and if your craft capsizes, swimming can become very important! It may be a good idea to take a few lessons at your local swim center if you are unfamiliar with proper form.

Underwater Swimming

Kayakers and canoeists should be able to hold their breath underwater for prolonged periods of time. It's important to train the lungs and the mind to be able to stay underwater, without panicking.

Wear a watch to keep track of your times when swimming underwater. Start with intervals of 15 to 30 seconds and slowly add more time with each workout. For safety, make these sessions close to shore or in a pool.

Chapter 5

Strength Training

Attitude is a little thing that makes a big difference.

Anonymous

Bursts of speed are often required when paddling. This is why strength training is a powerful component in your conditioning program. As mentioned earlier, strength training consists of relatively short bursts of muscular force anywhere between 1 second and 2 minutes. This type of training builds size and strength in the muscles and conditions them to store more energy for immediate use.

However, after only twenty or thirty seconds of such activity the source of immediate energy is exhausted and the muscles (and your liver) have to release a form of sugar that is broken down to create even more energy. Strength training conditions the body to store more of this sugar for future needs. This chemical reaction not only allows the muscles to continue generating force but also unfortunately creates lactic acid. Lactic acid accumulation in muscle tissue creates a burning sensation in the muscles. This burning may cause you to stop before you want. Strength training increases your tolerance for lactic acid, allowing you to paddle harder and farther. Other benefits of strength training include:

- Increased energy levels.

- Reduced injury potential.

- Increased bone density.

- Increased body circulation.
- Heightened body awareness.

When performing strength exercises, remember the five Rs, important elements of every strength program:

1. Resistance: The amount of weight or other resistance used during an exercise. Whatever the amount of resistance chosen, it's essential to retain proper form while doing the exercise.

2. Repetitions: The number of times a movement is performed during a set of an exercise. Typically, the lower the number of repetitions (with high resistance), the more basic strength is trained; the higher the repetitions (with low resistance), the more muscular endurance is trained.

3. Range of motion: The movement a muscle is responsible for. Ideally, it is best to train the muscle's fullest range of motion.

4. Rest: The amount of time spent resting between each set of exercises. An ideal rest period is between 30 seconds and 2 minutes, but the rest period may increase with greater intensity of exercise.

5. Recovery: The amount of time spent between strength training workouts of the same muscle group. It is often recommended that you allow 48 hours after strength training one muscle group before exercising that same group again, though this is not an iron-clad rule. If you find that you are strength training the same muscle groups two days in a row, it would be wise to change the selection of exercises for the following day (for example, when exercising the chest [pectorals], perform the dumbbell bench press on Monday and perform stability ball push-ups on Tuesday).

When you are training for strength, try to achieve temporary muscle fatigue in one set of each exercise. Temporary muscle fatigue occurs when the muscles are so exhausted that another repetition cannot be performed with proper technique.

It's important to maintain proper technique from start to finish in a set. It's equally important to have someone act as a spotter for safety when you perform exercises with weights that are suspended above your body.

Exhale during the exertion phase of each exercise (for example, exhaling as you push upward during the dumbbell bench press). If you experience dizziness or pain during an exercise, stop immediately and omit that exercise from the workout for the time being.

In selecting your strength workout program, choose a range of exercises that incorporate all the major muscle groups. If you intend to perform strength workouts more than three to four times per week, it may be better to focus on upper body on one day and lower body on a different day.

A word about weights: Use an amount of weight that permits you to properly perform a set of no less than 8 repetitions and no more than 15. If you are able to perform more than 15, increase the weight; if you can't do 8, consider decreasing the weight.

The exercises illustrated in this chapter provide details on how to perform them correctly, and you can refer back to these descriptions as you get into your training program. Exercises are divided into three categories: upper body; lower body; and torso. Each description lists the muscles that are involved in the exercise, and these muscles are shown in the Muscle Chart in appendix 4.

The workout programs in chapter 8 list suggested exercise schedules and provide the appropriate number of sets and repetitions.

Some of the following exercises require a workout facility with ample equipment and space to execute the drills safely, but other exercises can be performed at home. Therefore, even if you're not a member of a gym, you can still create an effective program of strength training.

Most of these exercises can be performed in a number of variations, which can be explained by gym staff trainers or others familiar with the routines.

Upper Body Exercises

External Rotation I

1. Lie on your left side with the bottom arm folded under your head for support and your legs slightly bent and parallel.

2. Bend the upper arm at a right angle, with the elbow pressed into your rib cage. [1]

3. Hold a dumbbell in that hand and exhale as you lift the dumbbell above the elbow. [2]

4. Inhale as you lower the dumbbell back to the starting position.

5. Repeat on the other side.

Muscles involved: Rotator cuff muscles.
Benefit: Encourages shoulder function and stabilization.

External Rotation II

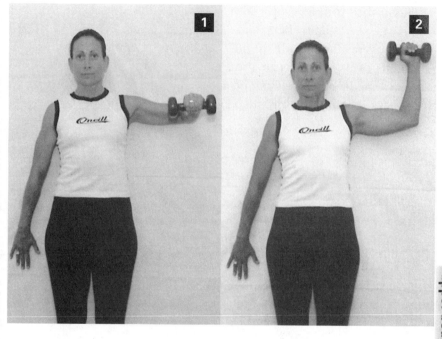

1. Stand with your feet parallel and hip-width apart.

2. With a dumbbell in your left hand, raise that elbow up to shoulder height out away from your body, with the dumbbell hanging down. Keep the elbow bent at a right angle (90 degrees); keep the upper arm at a right angle from the midline of your body. [1]

3. Keeping the elbow at shoulder height, exhale as you raise the dumbbell up directly above the elbow. [2]

4. Inhale as you lower the dumbbell back to the starting position.

5. Repeat, with the dumbbell in your right hand.

Muscles involved: Rotator cuff muscles.
Benefit: Encourages shoulder function and stabilization.

Lateral Raise

1. Stand with your feet hip-width apart, knees slightly bent, and weights resting outside of the thighs. (This exercise can also be performed from a kneeling position, as shown in the photos.) [1]

2. Exhale as you raise your arms to shoulder height. [2]

3. Inhale as you lower your arms to the starting position.

4. Do not allow your back to arch or your hips to move forward as the weights are lifted.

Muscle involved: Medial deltoid.
Benefit: Strengthens shoulder muscles.

rotator cuvv exercises

Upright Row

1. Stand with your feet parallel and hip-width apart, with knees slightly bent.

2. Hold dumbbells (or a barbell) in front of your thighs. [1]

3. Exhale as you bend your elbows and lift the dumbbells up just below your chin. [2]

4. Inhale as you return the dumbbells to the starting position.

Muscles involved: Upper trapezius, brachioradialis, posterior deltoid.

Benefit: Strengthens upper shoulder area.

Dumbbell Bench Press

1. Lie on your back on a bench, with your feet flat on the bench or a box or the floor.

2. Grip weights, with hands shoulder-width apart.

3. Inhale as you lower the weight until the elbows form a 90-degree angle. [1]

4. Exhale as you press the weight upward to the starting position. [2]

Muscles involved: Pectoralis major and minor, anterior and medial deltoid, triceps brachii.

Benefit: Strengthens front portion of torso.

upper body exercises

Dumbbell Pullover

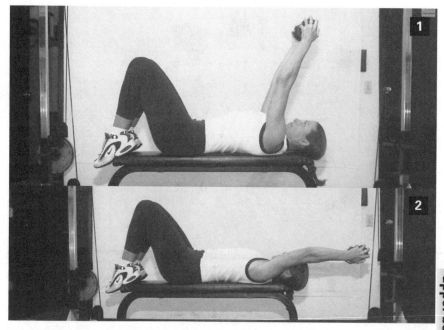

1. Lie on your back on a bench with feet on the bench, a box, or the floor.

2. Grip a dumbbell with both hands and with your arms straight above your head. [1]

3. Inhale as you lower the weight behind your head until your arms are parallel with the bench. [2]

4. Exhale as you raise the weight back to the starting position.

5. Keep abdominals firm at all times, with your lower back pressed into the bench.

Muscles involved: Pectoralis major, latissimus dorsi, triceps brachii, serratus anterior.

Benefit: Strengthens torso muscles involved in paddling.

Straight-Arm Pulldown

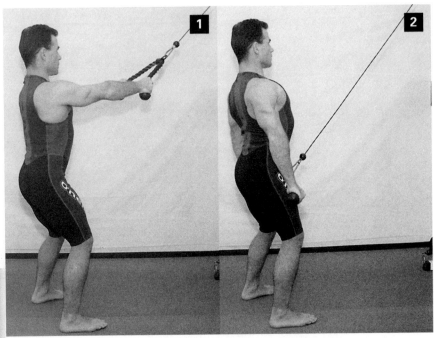

1. Bend your legs slightly, keeping your abdominals firm.

2. Keep your torso still.

3. Grasp the handles of the lat pulldown machine (also called a high pulley cable station) with a shoulder-width grip. [1]

4. Exhale as you pull the metal bar down to your thighs. [2]

5. Inhale as you raise your arms and return the bar to the starting position.

Muscles involved: Pectorals, latissimus dorsi, triceps brachii, serratus anterior, abdominals.

Benefit: Strengthens muscles involved in paddling.

Single Straight-Arm Pulldown

1. Bend your legs slightly, keeping your abdominals firm.

2. Keep your torso still.

3. Grip a handle in your right hand. [1]

4. Exhale as you pull the handle down to your right thigh. [2]

5. Inhale as you return your arm to the starting position.

6. Repeat, gripping with your left hand.

Muscles involved: Pectorals, latissimus dorsi, triceps brachii, serratus anterior, abdominals.

Benefit: Helps establish more balance with left and right arms.

Lat Pulldown

1. Get down on one knee, positioning the other foot forward.

2. Grasp the bar, with hands equidistant from the center. [1]

3. Your shoulders should be pulled slightly back behind the hips.

4. Exhale as you pull the bar down below your chin. [2]

5. Inhale as you return the bar to the starting position.

Major muscles involved: Latissimus dorsi, middle trapezius, rhomboids, posterior deltoid, biceps brachii, brachioradialis.

Benefit: Strengthens outer back and arms.

Seated Row

1. Sit in a tall position, with your knees slightly bent and your feet braced on opposite sides of the cable.

2. Grip the handles in a slightly forward seated posture. [1]

3. Exhale as your arms pull toward your body. [2]

4. Inhale as you use your arms to return the weight to the starting position.

5. At no time during the exercise should the upper body arch back behind the hips.

Major muscles involved: Latissimus dorsi, middle trapezius, rhomboids, posterior deltoid, biceps brachii, brachioradialis.
Benefit: Strengthens muscles responsible for rowing.

One-Arm Row

1. Rest your left hand and knee upon a bench, with the right leg slightly bent and planted firmly on the floor and a dumbbell held in the hand of your hanging right arm. [1]

2. With a neutral spine, exhale as you lift the weight up with your right arm to the side of your rib cage. [2]

3. Inhale as you lower the weight back to the starting position.

4. Change sides and repeat.

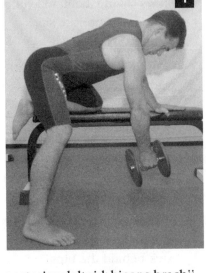

Muscles involved: Rhomboids, middle trapezius, latissimus dorsi, posterior deltoid, biceps brachii.
Benefit: Promotes balance of strength in both arms and torso.

Bent-Over Row

1. In a standing position, grasp a barbell with a shoulder-width grip.

2. Keeping your back straight, bend at the hips and knees until your torso is almost parallel to the floor.

3. The barbell should hang directly below your shoulders. [1]

4. Exhale as you pull the barbell to the center of your chest. [2]

5. Inhale as you return the barbell to the starting position.

6. Do not lift with the lower back muscles; those muscles should be contracting but not lifting.

Muscles involved: Rhomboids, middle trapezius, latissimus dorsi, posterior deltoid, biceps brachii.

Benefit: Builds strength for pulling and rowing.

Paddle Simulator

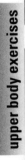

1. Grip the wooden rod as you would a canoe paddle. [1]

2. Exhale as you use both arms to pull the rod back so the bottom hand is past your hips. [2]

3. Inhale as you return the handle to the starting position. Perform exercise on both your left and right sides.

Muscles involved: Pectorals, latissimus dorsi, anterior and posterior deltoids, biceps brachii, triceps brachii.

Benefit: Strengthens body for overall paddling power.

Note: This exercise makes use of a wooden rod about 5 feet long, such as a shovel handle. The rod is fitted at one end with an eyebolt, which is then attached to the lower pulley of the cable station. You can make this device at home. [3]

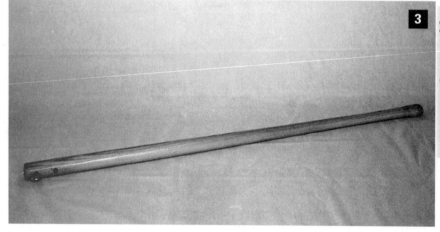

3

upper body exercises

Lower Body Exercises

Leg Press

1. Place your feet hip-width apart and parallel. Sit with your lower back in contact with the back rest of the leg press machine. [1]

2. Inhale as you lower the weight until your knees are at right angles. [2]

3. Keep abdominals firm, and your lower back pressed into the pad.

4. Exhale as you press the weight upward to the starting position.

5. Press evenly through the heels and balls of the feet at all times.

6. Do not lock the knee joints in a straight position at any time.

Muscles involved: Hamstrings, gluteals, quadriceps.
Benefit: Enhances leg and hip strength.

Lying Leg Curl

1. Lie on your stomach on the lying leg curl machine, with the back of your lower legs under the roller pad.

2. Hold on to the handles or chest pad and keep your head in a neutral position. [1]

3. Exhale as you bend your knees to lift the weight up to a right angle at the knee. [2]

4. Inhale as you lower the weight back to the starting position.

5. Do not hyperextend the knee at the bottom of the movement.

Muscles involved: Hamstrings.
Benefit: Strengthens the back of the legs.

Squat

1. Stand with feet hip-width apart or slightly wider.

2. Rest a barbell on your shoulders, just above the shoulder blades (not on your neck). [1]

3. Inhale as your body descends. Allow your hips and knees to bend, and keep your chest upright. [2]

4. Exhale as you return your body to the starting position.

5. Do not allow your hips to descend below the knees.

6. Weight should be placed on the heels.

7. Keep your head position neutral or slightly upward.

Muscles involved: Gluteals, hamstrings, quadriceps.
Benefit: Strengthens legs and torso while focusing on balance.

lower body exercises

Split Squat

1. Rest a barbell on your shoulders, just above the shoulder blades (not on the neck).

2. Step forward with your right foot, placing it about 3 feet ahead of your left foot. [1]

3. Inhale as you bend both legs at the knees and hips.

4. Lower your body until your left (rear) knee is an inch from the floor. [2]

5. Reverse direction and exhale until your legs are almost straight.

6. Repeat, with your left leg forward.

7. Do not let the forward knee bend past your toes; keep your shin and knee perpendicular to the ground.

Muscles involved: Quadriceps, hamstrings, gluteals, gastrocnemius.
Benefit: Strengthens legs in two positions while focusing on balance.

lower body exercises

Walking Lunge

1. Inhale as you take a step forward with your left foot.

2. Descend until your left knee is directly above your heel. [1]

3. Keep your shoulders directly above your hips at all times.

4. Exhale as your forward leg pulls and the rear leg pushes your body forward to a standing position. [2]

5. Be sure the hips and shoulders move forward at the same time.

6. Repeat, stepping forward with the right foot.

Muscles involved: Quadriceps, hamstrings, gluteals.
Benefit: Strengthens legs in forward motion while focusing on balance.

lower body exercises

Stiff Leg Deadlift

1. Stand tall, grasping a barbell (body bar) in front of your upper legs with both hands. [1]

2. Inhale as you lower the weight below your knees. [2]

3. Keep your back straight as your hips bend and move backward.

4. Exhale as you lift the weight back to the starting position.

5. Keep your back straight and do not lock out the knees.

Muscles involved: Hamstrings, gluteals.
Benefit: Strengthens back of hips and legs.

Torso Exercises

Knee Lifts

1. Support your body on both elbow pads. [1]

2. Exhale as you lift both legs, bent at right angles, upward.

3. Raise both legs until your knees almost touch your elbows. [2]

4. Inhale as you lower your legs back to the starting position.

Muscles involved: Psoas major, abdominals.
Benefit: Strengthens core muscles.
Note: The equipment needed for this exercise is found in most gyms. The straps are often referred to as ab straps.

torso exercises

Opposite Arm and Leg Raise

1. Lying face down, exhale as you lift your right arm and your left leg off the floor. [1]

2. Inhale as you lower the arm and leg back to the floor.

3. Repeat, using the left arm and right leg. [2]

Muscles involved: Gluteals, hamstrings, spinal erectors, deltoids, lower trapezius.

Benefit: Strengthens each side of lower back.

The Chop

1. Stand with your legs 3 feet apart, in a slight squat position.

2. With both hands, grab the handle of the upper pulley on a cable station. [1]

3. Keep your arms rigid but slightly bent at the elbow.

4. Exhale as you twist your waist and pull downward with both arms, to the left side of your body. [2]

5. Inhale as you twist your body back to the starting position.

6. Repeat, pulling downward to the right side.

7. Keep your arms in front of your torso as the body twists during the exercise.

Muscles involved: External and internal obliques, latissimus dorsi.
Benefit: Strengthens rotational muscles of the torso.

Twisting Lift

1. Stand with your legs 3 feet apart, in a slight squat position.

2. With both hands, grab the handle of the lower pulley on a cable station. [1]

3. Keep your arms rigid but slightly bent at the elbow.

4. Exhale as you twist your waist and pull upward with both arms, to the right side of your body. [2]

5. Inhale as you twist your body back to the starting position.

6. Repeat, pulling upward to the left side.

7. Keep your arms in front of your torso as the body twists during the exercise.

Muscles involved: External and internal obliques, latissimus dorsi.
Benefit: Strengthens rotational muscles of the torso.

Good Morning Exercise

1. Stand with your feet parallel, knees slightly bent and 2 feet apart. (You can place a barbell across the back of your shoulders during this exercise, but it might be wise to start with just your own body weight or to place a paddle across your shoulders before adding the weight of a barbell.) [1]

2. Inhale as you bend your body into the hips and lower your torso until your spine is parallel to the floor. [2]

3. Exhale as you lift your torso back to the starting position.

Muscles involved: spinal erectors, hamstrings, gluteals.
Benefit: Strengthens lower back and buttocks.

Abdominal Crunch

1. Lie on your back, with knees bent at right angles and feet flat.
2. Clasp your hands together and cradle the back of your head. [1]
3. Pinch your shoulder blades together.
4. Exhale as you lift up your shoulders and head. [2]
5. Inhale as you lower your body back to the floor.

Muscles involved: abdominals.
Benefit: Isolates and strengthens abdominal muscles.

Oblique Crunch

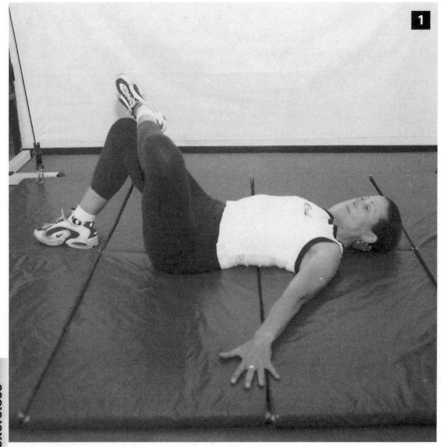

1. Lie on your back with your right hand cradling the back of your head.

2. Cross your left leg over the right knee. [1]

3. Exhale as you lift your right elbow and shoulder and twist in the direction of the crossed knee until the shoulder blade lifts off the floor. [2]

4. Inhale as you return to the starting position.

5. Repeat, using the opposite side.

Muscles involved: Abdominals, external and internal obliques.
Benefit: Creates a balance of strength in the torso.

Lateral Torso Lift

1. Lie on your left side with both legs together and the lower elbow propped under your shoulder. [1]

2. Exhale as you lift your hips off the floor until just the left foot remains on the floor; the leg should not touch the ground. [2]

3. Inhale as you lower your body back to the starting position.

4. Repeat, lying on your right side.

Muscles involved: Internal and external obliques.
Benefit: Strengthens the sides of the torso.

Bicycles

1. Lie on your back with hands clasped behind your head and elbows out away from your body.

2. Exhale as you pull up so that the right elbow touches the left knee. [1]

3. Repeat using the left elbow and the right knee. [2]

4. Inhale as you return to the starting position.

Muscles involved: Internal and external obliques, psoas major, abdominals.

Benefit: Strengthens core muscles responsible for rotation.

Chapter 6

Medicine Ball Training

Let me tell you the secret that has led me to my goal. My strength lies solely in my tenacity.

Louis Pasteur

Looking back at the history of fitness in America, it's hard not to laugh at some of the contraptions purported to be beneficial to good health—from the waist belt connected to a vibrating machine that was supposed to jiggle away unwanted pounds to the little electric shock pads that would jolt a beer belly into the abdomen of Adonis.

At least one fitness item, however, has stood the test of time and is now receiving new attention: the good old medicine ball. A medicine ball is simply a heavy ball used in performing various bending, throwing, lifting, and twisting movements. These movements mimic the torso action involved when paddling. It would be dangerous to play catch with a dumbbell but it can be a lot of fun with a medicine ball. Medicine balls, available at most sporting goods stores, come in all sizes and weights, from one pound to 25 pounds, and are stuffed with rags and sand to provide weight. Consider medicine ball exercises as another portion of the strength training part of your program. Exercises with a medicine ball are also a great way to warm up *all* the body's muscles.

Medicine ball movements require cooperation and coordination between the body's core muscles in the torso with those of the arms and legs. Medicine ball exercises are more functional and specific to everyday life because they focus on transferring force from the core to the rest of the body. Many of today's exercise machines fail to do this because they concentrate on isolating movements rather than on those that are more complex.

The following medicine ball exercises are great for paddlers. It might be wise to start with a 3-pound to 5-pound ball to help train the muscles in the proper movement before increasing intensity with heavier balls.

The exercises illustrated here will get you familiar with the routines and also serve as a reference once you've started your training program. The workout programs in chapter 8 include suggestions for incorporating medicine ball exercises into your strength training, with appropriate number of sets, repetitions, and rest times.

Choose two to four of the following exercises.

Axe Chop

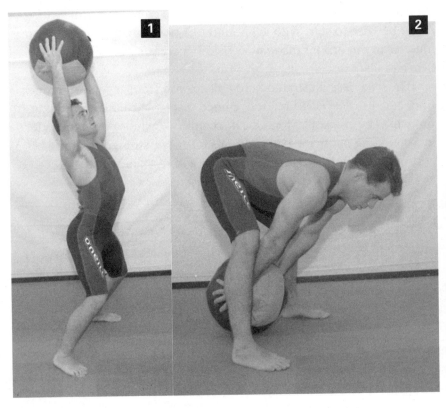

1. Stand with your feet parallel and hip-width apart.

2. Hold the medicine ball in both hands above your head. [1]

3. Exhale as you bend at the hips and use your torso and arms to lower the ball down between your ankles. [2]

4. Inhale as you return the ball to the starting position.

Benefit: Strengthens torso flexion and extension.

Seated Twist

1. Sit with your legs in front of your body, and your knees slightly bent so your heels dig into the floor.

2. Holding onto the ball with both hands, swing the ball to the left side of your body. [1]

3. Reverse direction to the other side. [2]

4. Keep your arms straight in front of your chest, as if frozen in that position, so that rotation occurs at the waist and not at the shoulders.

5. Make certain your head rotates with your torso.

Benefit: Strengthens torso rotation.

Russian Twist

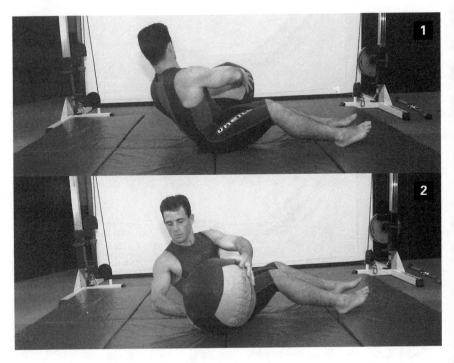

1. Sit with your knees bent and your heels on the floor.

2. Holding on to the ball with both hands, lean your torso back until it is at an angle of 45 degrees to the floor.

3. Swing the ball to the left side of your body. [1]

4. Reverse direction to the other side. [2]

5. Keep your arms straight in front of your chest, as if frozen in that position, so that rotation occurs at the waist and not at the shoulders.

6. Make certain your head also rotates with your torso.

Benefit: Strengthens torso rotation while engaging hip and abdominal muscles.

Overhead Toss

1. Lie on your back with knees bent at right angles.

2. With both hands over your head, grip the medicine ball. [1]

3. Exhale as you curl your body upward and hurl the ball forward. [2]

4. Inhale as you catch the ball when it is thrown back to you and as you lower back to the starting position.

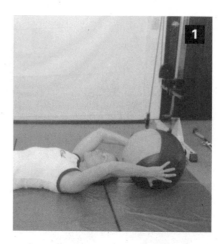

Benefit: Strengthens abdominals and torso flexion.

Note: You'll need a partner to catch and return the ball. Also, a trampoline-like device is available that is angled to bounce the ball back to the thrower.

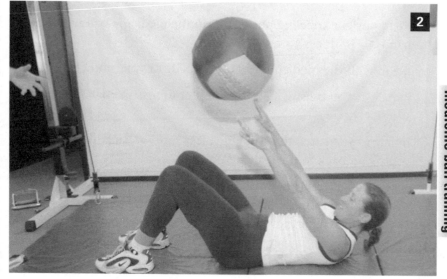

medicine ball training

Rotary Torso Toss

1. In an upright kneeling position, grip the medicine ball with both hands.

2. Begin with the medicine ball on one side of your body. [1]

3. Exhale as you twist your body in order to toss the ball to the opposite side. [2]

4. Inhale as you catch the ball when it is thrown back to you and as you swing back to the starting position.

Benefit: Strengthens rotational movement and the body's ability to transfer force from the torso to the upper and lower body.

Note: You'll need a partner to catch and return the ball.

medicine ball training

Chest Pass Crunch

1. Lie on your back with knees bent at right angles.

2. With both hands above your chest, grip the medicine ball. [1]

3. Exhale as you curl your body upward and hurl the ball forward. [2]

4. Inhale as you catch the ball when it is thrown back to you and as you lower back to the starting position.

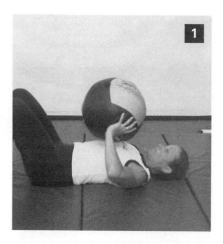

Benefit: Strengthens abdominals, upper body, and torso flexion.

Note: You'll need a partner to catch and return the ball. Also, a trampoline-like device is available that is angled to bounce the ball back to the thrower.

medicine ball training

Back Extension

1. Lie on your stomach with legs almost parallel.

2. Place the medicine ball against the back of your shoulders, with elbows pointing to the side, away from your body [1].

3. Inhale as you lift your torso until your chest is several inches off the floor [2].

4. Exhale as you lower your torso back to the starting position.

Benefit: Strengthens lower back and buttocks.

medicine ball training

Standing Torso Rotation

1. Stand in a forward split position, with one foot 2 to 3 feet ahead of the other foot.

2. Lower your body until your hips are at the same height as the front knee.

3. Hold the medicine ball with both hands and raise your arms away from your body, just below shoulder height.

4. Rotate through the hips as your arms swing left [1], and then right [2], and then back to the starting position.

5. The entire torso should rotate at the same time.

Benefit: Promotes balance and coordination with full body rotation.

Chapter 7

Stability Ball Training

To see one's goal and to drive toward it, steeling one's heart, is most uplifting.

Henrik Ibsen

Stability balls are inflatable rubber balls that resemble the old "hippity-hoppity" toys we bounced around on as children. The main difference is that the stability ball does not have a handle. Stability balls come in different sizes, from 2 feet in diameter on up.

The purpose of exercising with these balls is to enhance the body's balance, core strength, and ability to maintain stability. When exercising on an unstable surface, the muscle groups or muscles that provide stability (the rotator cuff, abdominals, and lower back) become more active.

The more stable the body, the less likely an injury. A crude analogy of the difference between weak and strong stabilizing muscles would be a house kept together with staples compared to one held with six-inch nails. Many traditional strength training exercises (e.g. bench press, bicep curls) do not address the stabilizing muscles. The exercise merely demands sheer force from the body any way it can be created. Therefore it is essential that other exercises be incorporated to address the stabilizing muscles.

Some of these stability ball exercises may appear gentle in comparison to other strength exercises (e.g. squats, lunges) but they nevertheless focus on strengthening muscles and should be considered part of your strength training program. Many of the targeted muscles are small and do not demand tremendous amounts of work. Nor will these exercises make you out of breath. Nevertheless, these stability ball exercises are extremely important in maintaining proper stability.

The exercises illustrated here will introduce you to the stability ball and serve as a reference once you've started your training program. When performing the exercises, be sure to have ample space free of sharp or hard objects in case you lose your balance.

The workout programs in chapter 8 include suggestions for incorporating stability ball exercises into your strength training, with appropriate number of sets, repetitions, and rest times.

Choose two to four of the following exercises.

Abdominal Crunch

1. Lie on your back on the stability ball, with your feet placed on a wall or flat on the floor.

2. Cradle your head with both hands, with shoulder blades pinched together. [1]

3. Exhale as you curl your torso upward; your spine should be at 30 degrees of flexion; the lower back should not lift off the ball. [2]

4. Inhale as you lower your torso back to the starting position.

Benefit: Strengthens abdominals while maintaining balance.

Walk-out

1. Sit on top of the ball with your feet flat, pointing straight ahead, and your arms straight out at shoulder height. [1]

2. Lean back and curl your spine forward as your feet walk out.

3. Keep thighs, hips, and spine parallel to the floor as your feet walk out until your shoulders, neck, and back of the head are resting on top of the ball. [2]

4. Reverse direction, walking back until you are seated in the starting position.

Benefit: Strengthens abdominals, hips, and lower back while maintaining balance.

stability ball training

Trunk (Torso) Rotation

1. Begin in the walk-out position, with hips, thighs, and spine parallel to the floor, and shoulders, neck, and back of the head resting on top of the stability ball.

2. Clasp your hands together, with arms straight above your chest. [1]

3. Exhale as you twist your torso to the left until your left arm becomes parallel to the floor.

4. Inhale as you twist your torso back to the starting position.

5. Exhale as you repeat the movement to the right. [2]

6. Inhale as you twist your torso back to the starting position.

Benefit: Strengthens rotational muscles while promoting balance.

Push-Up

1. Lie face down on the stability ball and place both hands forward on the floor.

2. Keep your body rigid as your hands walk forward until the thighs are on top of the ball and the torso is supported with the arms. The ball should end up between your knees and ankles.

3. Inhale as you lower your body until the chest is an inch off the floor. [1]

4. Exhale as you press your body upward to the starting position. [2]

Benefit: Strengthens upper body and rotator cuff while increasing stability of the torso.

Note: To increase exercise intensity, walk your body out so only your feet are on top of the ball when performing the push upward.

stability ball training

The Pike

1. Lie face down on the stability ball and place both hands forward on the floor.

2. Keep your body rigid as your hands walk forward until the lower legs are on top of the ball and the torso is supported with the arms. [1]

3. Exhale as you raise your body by bending and lifting at the hips.

4. Keep the spine straight at all times.

5. Pause once your hips lift directly above your shoulders. [2]

6. Inhale as you lower your body in a controlled manner back to the starting position.

Benefit: Strengthens upper body, hips, and torso while reinforcing shoulder stability.

stability ball training

Lateral Flexion

1. Lie on the stability ball on the left side of your body.

2. Brace your right foot on the floor behind you, with your left foot about 3 feet out in front of the right foot.

3. Place your hands behind your head, with elbows out away from your body. [1]

4. Exhale as you bend your torso upward off the ball. Press down your body's weight to keep the ball from moving. [2]

5. Inhale as you return to the starting position.

6. Alternate sides.

Benefit: Strengthens external and internal obliques while focusing on balance.

Back Extension

1. Lie stomach down on the stability ball, with your feet anchored against a wall and the ball positioned under hips and stomach.

2. Place your hands behind your head, with elbows out. [1]

3. Exhale as you raise your body to a straight position; do not arch your back. Press down your body's weight to keep the ball from moving. [2]

4. Inhale as you lower your body back to the starting position.

Benefit: Strengthens lower back and buttocks while maintaining balance.

stability ball training

Back Extension with Twist

1. Lie stomach down on the stability ball, with your feet anchored against a wall and the ball positioned under hips and stomach.

2. Place your hands behind your head, with elbows out.

3. Exhale as you raise and twist your body to a position where one shoulder is higher than the other; do not arch your back. [1]

4. Inhale as you lower your body back to the starting position.

5. Repeat, raising the opposite shoulder. [2]

Benefit: Strengthens lower back rotation while maintaining balance.

stability ball training

Kneeling with Arms Raised

1. Start by positioning your body on top of the stability ball with hands and knees.

2. Raise your upper body and release the hand position as you pull your knees forward and under your body.

3. Keep your body upright while balancing on your knees and lower legs. [1]

4. Exhale as you raise your arms above your head. [2]

5. Inhale as you lower your arms back to your sides.

Benefit: Reinforces core stability and body balance.

Note: Be careful: this is an advanced balancing exercise. Once confidence and coordination have been established, this balance position can be substituted for many standing dumbbell exercises.

Chapter 8

Sample Workout Programs

Now that all the components of the paddler's conditioning program have been discussed in detail it is time to put your program together. The sample workouts given in this chapter will help you create your program. The workouts each have three parts: flexibility, endurance, and strength. Although the flexibility portion appears first remember that most gains occur when stretching is performed at the end of a workout. The routines are made up of lying, sitting, kneeling, and standing stretches. Be sure to select a few stretches from each group with each program you design. Also the Sun Salutation is not included with the samples. Instead use the Sun Salutation as a wake-up routine as often as possible. It will increase your flexibility and energize you first thing in the morning.

The endurance program is a blend of land and water exercises. Depending on weather and water conditions at times you may be forced to use more land endurance exercises but, if possible, create a blend. Labels of "Low," "Moderate," and "High" are given to describe the intensity level of an exercise. "Low" refers to 60–70 percent of maximum heart rate and 5–6 on the scale of the Rate of Perceived Exertion (R.P.E.). "Moderate" is 70–80 percent of maximum heart rate and 6–7 on the R.P.E. scale. "High" refers to 80–90 percent of maximum heart rate and 7–9 on the R.P.E. scale.

The strength program is a combination of upper body, lower body, and torso exercises. Stability ball and medicine ball exercises are also included. If you have the use of these exercise balls incorporate them into your routine as often as possible. If not, create as much variety in the other exercises as possible. Focus on the exercises that are challenging. Too often people focus on the exercises that are their "strong suits." They perform these exercises more than any others which creates strength imbalances (one muscle stronger than its counterpart). Imbalances lead to improper movement, and improper movements increase the chance of injury. Part of this approach is to *find* the exercises that are challenging. The true challenge is not to bench press 300 pounds; rather it is to find the weaker muscles and improve their strength.

Not all exercises appearing in this book are included in the sample routines. I didn't want you to simply copy my routines. Be original! Be creative! Hopefully enough variety and information has been provided so you can create your own program. Refer as often as you like to the photos and descriptions of the various exercises earlier in the book. The flexibility exercises are in chapter 2; endurance exercises in chapter 4; strength exercises in chapter 5; medicine ball exercises in chapter 6; and stability ball exercises in chapter 7. See appendix 1 for a list of all exercises. See the index to locate the page number for a specific exercise.

Home Program

Gyms and health clubs aren't your cup of tea? Too many muscleheads? Too much fluorescent spandex? Whatever the issue don't worry, you do not have to join the sweatshops. The following sample routines can be performed in the comfort and privacy of your home. It may not be a bad idea to invest in a few dumbbells, a medicine ball, and perhaps a stability ball. This will increase the number of exercises you can choose from.

Home Program: Weeks 1 and 2

Flexibility Training: 3–6 days per week

Exercise Work Schedule	
Elbow Presses	2 x 25 times
Pullovers	2 x 25 times
Crossover Twist	1 min.
Mad Cat Stretch	25 times
Seated Torso Twist	30 sec./side
Seated Lower-back Stretch	30 sec./side
Side Reach	30 sec./side
Wall Sit	30 sec.

Endurance Training: 3–5 days per week

Type	Work/Duration	Intensity
Walking	20 min.	Low
Resistance Paddling	10 min.	Moderate

Strength Training: 2–3 days per week

Rest 30 seconds to one minute between sets.

Exercise	Sets	Repetitions
External Rotation I	1–3	10–12
Abdominal Crunch	2–3	15–25
Walk-out (Stability Ball)	2–3	5–10
Push-up (Stability Ball)	1–3	8–12
Axe Chop (Medicine Ball)	1–3	8–12
Seated Twist (Medicine Ball)	1–3	8–12
Upright Row	1–3	8–12
Dumbbell Pullover	1–3	8–12
Split Squat	1–3	8–12

Home Program: Weeks 3 and 4

Flexibility Training: 3–6 days per week

Exercise Work Schedule	
Crossed Knee Lift	30 sec./side
Crossover Twist	30 sec./side
Hamstring Stretch with Strap	30 sec./side
Crossed Arm Stretch	30 sec./side
Arm Circles	2 x 25 times/direction
Downward-facing Dog	1 min.
Modified Hurdler Stretch	30 sec./side
Triangle Pose	30 sec./side
Reverse Triangle Pose	30 sec./side
Wrist Stretch	2 x 30 sec.

Endurance Training: 3–5 days per week

Type	Work/Duration	Intensity
Interval Paddling	10 x 1 min.	Moderate/High
Swimming	20 min.	Moderate

Strength Training: 3–4 days per week

Rest 30 seconds to one minute between sets.

Exercise	Sets	Repetitions
External Rotation II	2–3	8–15
Trunk Rotation (Stability Ball)	2–3	15–20
Lateral Flexion (Stability Ball)	2–3	15–20
Russian Twist (Medicine Ball)	2–3	10–20
Back Extension (Medicine Ball)	2–3	10–20
Bicycles	2–3	8–15
One-arm Row	2–3	8–15
Dumbbell Bench Press	2–3	8–15
Walking Lunge	2–3	8–15
Squat	2–3	8–15

Home Program: Weeks 5 and 6

Flexibility Training: 3–6 days per week

Exercise	Work Schedule
I.T. Band Stretch with Strap	1 min./leg
Calf Stretch with Strap	1 min./leg
Crocodile Twist	1 min./side
Shoulder Pivots	2 x 30 times
Modified Shoulder Stand	1 min.
Simple Twist	1 min./side
The Frog	1 min.
Warrior Pose	1 min./side
Chest and Shoulder Stretch	1 min.
Downward-facing Dog	2 min.

Endurance Training: 3–5 days per week

Type	Work/Duration	Intensity
Back-Paddling	20 min.	Moderate
Land Paddle with Bands	10 min.	Moderate
Stair Climbing	10 x 50 steps	Moderate/High

Strength Training: 3–4 days per week

Rest 30 seconds to one minute between sets.

Exercise	Sets	Repetitions
Lateral Raise	3–4	8–15
The Pike (Stability Ball)	3–4	8–15
Back Extension with Twist (Stability Ball)	3–4	10–20
Standing Torso Rotation (Medicine Ball)	3–4	8–15
Overhead Toss (Medicine Ball)	3–4	8–15
Oblique Crunch	3–4	15–25
Lateral Torso Lift	3–4	15–20
Stiff Leg Deadlift	3–4	8–15
Bent-over Row	3–4	8–15
Dumbbell Pullover	3–4	8–15

Home Program: Weeks 7 and 8

Flexibility Training: 3–6 days per week

Exercise	Work Schedule
Superhero	2 x 30 sec.
Upper Spinal Floor Twist	1 min./side
Shoulder Pivots	3 x 25 times
Arm Circles	2 x 30 times/direction
Boat Pose	2 x 1 min.
Seated Lower-back Stretch	1 min./side
Hamstring Stretch with Strap	2 x 1 min./leg
Bar Hang	2 x 30 sec.
Warrior Pose	1 min./side
Triangle Pose	1 min./side

Endurance Training: 3–5 days per week

Type	Work/Duration	Intensity
Drafting Paddle	20 min.	Moderate/High
Underwater Swimming	10 x 30 sec.	Moderate/High
Running	20 min.	Moderate/High

Strength Training: 3–4 days per week

Rest 30 seconds to one minute between sets.

Exercise	Sets	Repetitions
Back Extension (Stability Ball)	3–4	15–25
Push-up (Stability Ball)	3–4	15–25
Chest Pass Crunch (Medicine Ball)	3–4	15–25
Axe Chop (Medicine Ball)	3–4	15–25
External Rotation I	3–4	15–20
One-arm Row	3–4	10–15
Upright Row	3–4	10–15
Walking Lunge	3–4	15–25
Abdominal Crunch	6–8	20–30
Bicycles	6–8	30–50

Home Program: Weeks 9 and 10

Flexibility Training: 3–6 days per week

Exercise	Work Schedule
Crossed Knee Lift	1 min./side
Crossover Twist	1 min./side
Mad Cat Stretch	30 times
Upward-facing Dog	1 min.
Side Lateral Raise	2 x 25 times
Modified Shoulder Stand	2 min.
Sitting Floor	1 min.
Reverse Triangle Pose	1 min./side
Advanced Shoulder Stretch	1 min./side
Wall Sit	2 min.

Endurance Training: 3–5 days per week

Type	Work/Duration	Intensity
Paddle Relay	3 relays at 100 yards	High
Water Sprints	8 x 50 yards	High
Stair Climbing	10 x 50 steps	Moderate/High

Strength Training: 3–4 days per week

Rest 30 seconds to one minute between sets.

Exercise	Sets	Repetitions
The Pike (Stability Ball)	3–4	10–15
Kneeling with Arms Raised (Stability Ball)	3–4	10–15
Rotary Torso Toss (Medicine Ball)	3–4	15–25
Overhead Toss (Medicine Ball)	4–6	20–30
External Rotation II	3–5	15–20
Dumbbell Bench Press	4–6	8–15
Bent-over Row	4–6	8–15
Opposite Arm and Leg Raise	4–6	15–25
Split Squat	4–6	8–15
Lateral Torso Lift	4–6	20–30

Gym Program

Are you a member of a gym? Thinking of joining one in the near future? The following routines are samples of what your gym routine might look like. Some machines may look different than the ones featured in this book. If you are unsure of the equipment be certain to ask a staff member for help.

One more thing: gym etiquette. Please carry a workout towel to wipe your perspiration off machines and allow other members to share equipment you are using when you are between sets. Your fellow gym members will thank you.

Gym Program: Weeks 1 and 2

Flexibility Training: 3–6 days per week

Exercise	Work Schedule
Elbow Presses	2 x 25 times
Hamstring Stretch with Strap	1 min./leg
Calf Stretch with Strap	1 min./leg
Arm Circles	25 times/direction
Sitting Floor	1 min.
Seated Lower-back Stretch	30 sec./side
Side Reach	30 sec./side

Endurance Training: 3–5 days per week

Type	Work/Duration	Intensity
Walking	20 min.	Low
Rowing Machine	10 min.	Moderate

Strength Training: 3–4 days per week

Rest 30 seconds to one minute between sets.

Exercise	Sets	Repetitions
Abdominal Crunch (Stability Ball)	2–3	10–20
Walk-out (Stability Ball)	2–3	5–15
Seated Twist (Medicine Ball)	2–3	10–20
Back Extension (Medicine Ball)	2–3	8–12
External Rotation I	2–3	8–12
Dumbbell Bench Press	2–3	8–12
Straight-arm Pulldown	2–3	8–12
Leg Press	2–3	8–12

Gym Program: Weeks 3 and 4

Flexibility Training: 3–6 days per week

Exercise	Work	Schedule
Crossed Knee Lift	30 sec./side	
Crossover Twist	30 sec./side	
Mad Cat Stretch	30 times	
Shoulder Pivots	30 times	
The Frog	30 sec.	
Modified Hurdler Stretch	30 sec./side	
Bar Hang	30 sec.	
Warrior Pose	30 sec./side	
Wall Sit	30 sec.	

Endurance Training: 3–5 days per week

Type	Work/Duration	Intensity
Resistance Paddling	10 min.	Moderate
Swimming	20 min.	Moderate
Rowing Machine	10 min.	Moderate

Strength Training: 3–4 days per week

Rest 30 seconds to one minute between sets.

Exercise	Sets	Repetitions
Lateral Flexion (Stability Ball)	2–3	15–25
Trunk Rotation (Stability Ball)	2–3	10–20
Axe Chop (Medicine Ball)	2–3	10–20
Overhead Toss (Medicine Ball)	2–3	10–20
Lateral Raise	2–3	8–12
Lat Pulldown	2–3	8–12
Seated Row	2–3	8–12
Squat	2–3	8–12
Opposite Arm and Leg Raise	2–3	15–25
Bicycles	3–4	20–30

Gym Program: Weeks 5 and 6

Flexibility Training: 3–6 days per week

Exercise	Work Schedule
Superhero	2 x 30 sec.
Crocodile Twist	1 min./side
Crossover Twist	1 min./side
Crossed Arm Stretch	1 min./side
Modified Shoulder Stand	1 min.
Boat Pose	1 min.
Seated Torso Twist	1 min./side
Triangle Pose	1 min./side
Reverse Triangle Pose	1 min./side
Wrist Stretch	1 min.

Endurance Training: 3–5 days per week

Type	Work/Duration	Intensity
Interval Paddling	10 x 1 min.	Moderate/High
Suicide Drills	3 sets	High
Running	20 min.	Moderate

Strength Training: 3–4 days per week

Rest 30 seconds to one minute between sets.

Exercise	Sets	Repetitions
Abdominal Crunch (Stability Ball)	4–6	25–40
Back Extension (Stability Ball)	4–6	15–30
Russian Twist (Medicine Ball)	3–4	10–20
Rotary Torso Toss (Medicine Ball)	3–4	10–20
External Rotation II	3–4	8–12
Single Straight-Arm Pulldown	3–4	8–12
Bent-Over Row	3–4	8–12
Walking Lunge	3–4	10–15
The Chop	3–4	10–15
Lateral Torso Lift	3–4	15–20

Gym Program: Weeks 7 and 8

Flexibility Training: 3–6 days per week

Exercise	Work Schedule
Crossed Knee Lift	1 min./side
Crossover Twist	1 min./side
Side Lateral Raise	25 times
Arm Circles	25 times/direction
Shoulder Pivots	25 times
Simple Twist	1 min./side
Seated Lower-back Stretch	1 min./side
Chest and Shoulder Stretch	1 min./side
Bar Hang	45 sec.
Advanced Shoulder Stretch	1 min./side

Endurance Training: 3–5 days per week

Type	Work/Duration	Intensity
Partner Towing	15 x 2 min.	Moderate/High
Underwater Swimming	10 x 30 sec.	Moderate
Stair Climbing	8 x 50 steps	Moderate

Strength Training: 3–4 days per week

Rest 30 seconds to one minute between sets.

Exercise	Sets	Repetitions
Push-up (Stability Ball)	3–4	10–20
Back Extension with Twist (Stability Ball)	3–4	10–20
Chest Pass Crunch (Medicine Ball)	3–4	15–25
Standing Torso Rotation (Medicine Ball)	3–4	10–20
External Rotation I	3–4	10–15
Upright Row	3–4	8–12
One-arm Row	3–4	8–12
Paddle Simulator	4–6	12–20
Split Squat	3–4	8–12
Knee Lifts	4–6	15–25

Gym Program: Weeks 9 and 10

Flexibility Training: 3–6 days per week

Exercise	Work Schedule
I.T. Band Stretch with Strap	1 min./side
Upward-facing Dog	2 x 30 sec.
Upper Spinal Floor Twist	1 min./side
Crossed Arm Stretch	1 min./side
Modified Shoulder Stand	2 min.
Downward-facing Dog	2 x 1 min.
Simple Twist	1 min./side
Boat Pose	2 x 1 min.
Triangle Pose	1 min./side
Reverse Triangle Pose	1 min./side

Endurance Training: 3–5 days per week

Type	Work/Duration	Intensity
Land Paddle with Bands	10 min.	Moderate
Drafting Paddle	30 min.	High
Swimming	20 min.	Moderate

Strength Training: 3–4 days per week

Rest 30 seconds to one minute between sets.

Exercise	Sets	Repetitions
Push-up (Stability Ball)	4–6	10–20
The Pike (Stability Ball)	4–6	8–15
Overhead Toss (Medicine Ball)	4–6	15–30
Standing Torso Rotation (Medicine Ball)	4–6	10–20
External Rotation II	3–4	10–20
Bent-over Row	3–4	8–15
Paddle Simulator	4–6	15–20
Stiff Leg Deadlift	3–4	8–12
Good Morning Exercise	3–4	10–20
Abdominal Crunch	4–6	20–30

Overnight Campground Routine

Since you have been conditioning your body at home or in the gym the weekend trip down the river is not enough exercise to challenge your already fine-tuned muscles. Here is a sample fitness program that will allow you to continue your fitness routine while everyone else goes to bed early and wakes up late. Remember you can always break out a paddling drill when no one is looking.

Flexibility Training: 3–6 days per week

Exercise	Work Schedule
Crossed Knee Lift	1 min./side
Crossover Twist	1 min./side
Mad Cat Stretch	30 times
Shoulder Pivots	30 times
Arm Circles	30 times/direction
Triangle Pose	30 sec./side
Reverse Triangle Pose	30 sec./side
Warrior Pose	30 sec./side
Upward-facing Dog	2 x 30 sec.
Downward-facing Dog	2 x 1 min.

Endurance Training: 3–5 days per week

Type	Duration	Intensity
Walking	20 min.	Low
Swimming	15 min.	Moderate
Underwater Swimming	10 x 30 sec.	Moderate

Strength Training: 3–4 days per week

Rest 30 seconds to one minute between sets.

Exercise	Sets	Repetitions
Lateral Raise	3–4	8–12
Push-up (Stability Ball)	3–4	10–20
Split Squat	3–4	10–15
Walking Lunge	3–4	10–15
Wall Sit	1–3	1 min.
Abdominal Crunch	3–4	15–25
Oblique Crunch	3–4	15–25
Opposite Arm and Leg Raise	3–4	15–25
Bicycles	3–4	20–30
Lateral Torso Lift	3–4	10–20

Appendix 1

Exercises at a Glance

Following is a list of all exercises described in this book, categorized by whether they are aimed mainly at promoting flexibility, endurance, or strength. You can use this list in personalizing your workouts, selecting from a variety of these exercises in adapting the workout programs in chapter 8 to suit your particular conditioning goals.

Check the chapters indicated in order to review the photos and descriptions of any of these exercises.

Flexibility Exercises

Lying Stretches (choose 2 to 4)

In chapter 2:

Elbow Presses
Pullovers
Crossed Knee Lift
Crossover Twist
Hamstring Stretch with Strap
Calf Stretch with Strap
I.T. Band (Iliotibial Band) Stretch
    with Strap
Superhero
Upward-facing Dog
Upper Spinal Floor Twist
Crocodile Twist

Kneeling Stretches (choose 2 to 4)

In chapter 2:

Mad Cat Stretch
Crossed Arm Stretch
Arm Circles
Shoulder Pivots
Side Lateral Raise
Modified Shoulder Stand
Downward-facing Dog

Sitting Stretches (choose 2 to 4)

In chapter 2:

The Frog
Boat Pose
Sitting Floor
Modified Hurdler Stretch
Seated Torso Twist
Simple Twist
Seated Lower-back Stretch

Standing Stretches (choose 2 to 4)

In chapter 2:

Bar Hang
Chest and Shoulder Stretch
Triangle Pose
Warrior Pose
Side Reach
Reverse Triangle Pose

Wall Sit
Wrist Stretch
Advanced Shoulder Stretch

In chapter 3:
Sun Salutation (series of stretches)

Endurance Exercises

Paddling Activities to Build Endurance (choose 1 to 3 for each workout session)

In chapter 4:
Resistance Paddling
Paddling Upstream
Interval Paddling
Partner Towing
Drafting Paddle
Tug-of-War
Back-paddling
Paddle Relays

Other Activities to Build Endurance (choose at least one, once a week)

In chapter 4:
Land Paddle with Resistance Bands
Rowing Machine
Suicide Drills
Water Sprints
Swimming
Underwater Swimming
Walking and Running

Stair Climbing
Drafting Runs and Cycling

Strength Exercises

Rotator Cuff Exercises (choose 1 to 2)

In chapter 5:
External Rotation I
External Rotation II
Lateral Raise

Body Exercises (choose 2 to 4)

In chapter 5:
Upright Row
Dumbbell Bench Press
Dumbbell Pullover
Straight-Arm Pulldown
Single Straight-Arm Pulldown
Lat Pulldown
Seated Row
One-Arm Row
Bent-Over Row
Paddle Simulator

In chapter 7 (stability ball):
Push-Up

Lower Body Exercises (choose 1 to 3)

In chapter 5:
Leg Press
Lying Leg Curl

Squat
Split Squat
Walking Lunge
Stiff Leg Deadlift

Torso Exercises (choose 3 to 5)

In chapter 5:

Knee Lifts
Opposite Arm and Leg Raise
The Chop
Twisting Lift
Good Morning Exercise
Abdominal Crunch
Oblique Crunch
Lateral Torso Lift
Bicycles

In chapter 6 (medicine ball):

Axe Chop
Seated Twist

Russian Twist
Overhead Toss
Rotary Torso Toss
Chest Pass Crunch
Back Extension
Standing Torso Rotation

In chapter 7 (stability ball):

Abdominal Crunch
Walk-out
Trunk (Torso) Rotation
Push-Up
The Pike
Lateral Flexion
Back Extension
Back Extension with Twist
Kneeling with Arms Raised

Workout Log

Rocky's Functional Integrative Training

Workout #1	Workout #2	Workout #3

Cardiovascular Conditioning Target Heart Rate = ____ beats/min.

Type of exercise	prog	int	dur	Type of exercise	prog	int	dur	Type of exercise	prog	int	dur
1 Interval Paddling	10 x 1 min	MED	30 min	1 Back Paddle		MED	20	1 Drafting Paddle		High	40 min
2 Swimming		MED	20 min	2 Rowing Machine	RACE MED		15 min	2 Underwater Swim	INTERVAL	MED	20 min
3 Water Sprints		HIGH	10 min	3 Stair Climbing	INTERVAL MED		10 min	3 Running		High	30 min

Strength Training ___ sets x ___ reps

Type of exercise	set1	set2	set3	Type of exercise	set1	set2	set3	Type of exercise	set1	set2	set3
1 External Rotation	3lb/15	3lb/12	5lb/10	1 Lateral Raise	5lb/15	5/15	5/15	1 Push Up w/ Stability Ball	Body/15	Body/12	Body/10
2 Trunk Rotation w/ Stability Ball	Body/15	Body/12	Body/10	2 The Pike w/ Stability Ball	Body/15	Body/15	Body/15	2 Kneeling on Stability Ball	Body/1min	Body/1min	Body/1min
3 Lateral Flexion w/ Stability Ball	Body/15	Body/12	Body/10	3 Back Ext. w/ Twist (Stability Ball)	Body/15	Body/15	Body/15	3 Rotary Torso Toss w/ Medicine Ball	8/15	10/15	12/15
4 Russian Twist w/ Medicine Ball	10lb/15	10lb/15	10lb/15	4 Torso Rotation w/ Medicine Ball	8/15	10/12	12/10	4 Overhead Toss w/ Medicine Ball	8/15	10/15	12/12
5 Back Extension w/ Medicine Ball	12/15	12/15	12lb/15	5 Overhead Toss w/ Medicine Ball	8/15	10/12	12/16	5 External Rotation II	5/15	5/15	5/15
6 Bicycles	Body/20	Body/20	Body/20	6 Oblique Crunch	Body/20	Body/20	Body/20	6 Dumbbell Bench Press	20/15	25/12	30/10
7 One Arm Row	15/15	20/12	25/10	7 Lateral Torso Lift	Body/20	Body/20	Body/20	7 Bent Over Row	30/15	35/12	40/10
8 Dumbbell Bench Press	30/15	35/12	40/10	8 Stiff-Leg Deadlift	20/15	25/12	30/10	8 Opposite Arm & Leg Raises	Body/15	Body/15	Body/15
9 Walking Lunge	20lb/15	25lb/15	30lb/15	9 Bent Over Row	20/15	25/12	30/10	9 Split Squat	10/15	15/12	20/10
10 Squat	95/15	105/12	115/10	10 Dumbbell Pullover	15/15	20/12	25/10	10 Lateral Torso Lift	Body/20	Body/20	Body/20

Flexibility Training hold each pose for 1-3 x 10-20 sec.

Workout #1	Workout #2	Workout #3
1 Crossed Knee Lift	1 I.T. Band Stretch w/ Strap	1 Upper Spinal Floor Twist
2 Crossover Twist	2 Calf Stretch w/ Strap	2 Shoulder Pivots
3 Hamstring Stretch w/Strap	3 Crocodile Twist	3 Arm Circles
4 Crossed Arm Stretch	4 Shoulder Pivots	4 Boat Pose
5 Arm Circles	5 Modified Shoulder Stand	5 Seated Low Back Stretch
6 Modified Hurdler's Stretch	6 Simple Twist	6 Bar Hang
7 Triangle Pose	7 Chest/Shoulder Stretch	7 Warrior Pose
8 Downward Dog	8 Downward Dog	8 Triangle Pose

Rocky's Functional Integrative Training

Workout #1	Workout #2	Workout #3

Cardiovascular Conditioning   Target Heart Rate = _____ beats/min.

Type of exercise	prog	int	dur	Type of exercise	prog	int	dur	Type of exercise	prog	int	dur
1				1				1			
2				2				2			
3				3				3			

Strength Training   _____ sets x _____ reps

Type of exercise	set1	set2	set3	Type of exercise	set1	set2	set3	Type of exercise	set1	set2	set3
1				1				1			
2				2				2			
3				3				3			
4				4				4			
5				5				5			
6				6				6			
7				7				7			
8				8				8			
9				9				9			
10				10				10			

Flexibility Training   hold each pose for 1-3 x 10-20 sec.

1	1	1
2	2	2
3	3	3
4	4	4
5	5	5
6	6	6
7	7	7
8	8	8

Appendix 3

Resources

Alter, Michael J. *Sport Stretch.* 2nd ed. Champaign IL: Human Kinetics, 1998.

Baechle, Thomas R., and Roger Earle, eds. *Essentials of Strength Training and Conditioning.* 2nd ed. Champaign IL: Human Kinetics, 2000.

Couch, Jean. *The Runner's Yoga Book: A Balanced Approach to Fitness.* Berkeley: Rodmell Press, 1990.

Horrigan, Joseph, D.C., and Jerry Robinson. *The 7-Minute Rotator Cuff Solution.* Los Angeles: Health for Life, 1991.

Muscle Balance and Function Development, www.dpdc-mbf.com

Appendix 4

Muscle Chart

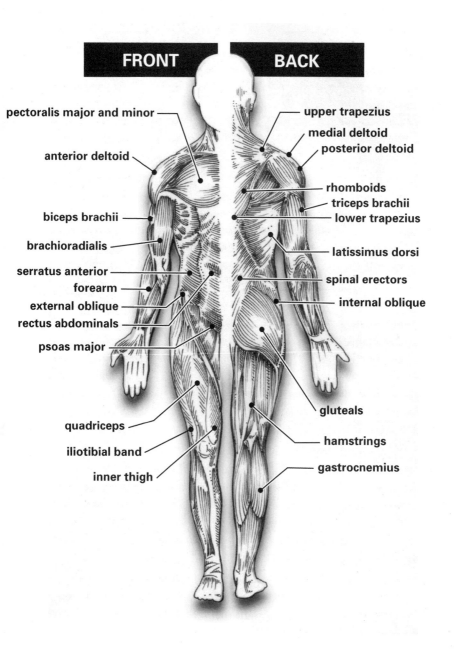

FRONT

BACK

pectoralis major and minor

anterior deltoid

biceps brachii

brachioradialis

serratus anterior

forearm

external oblique

rectus abdominals

psoas major

quadriceps

iliotibial band

inner thigh

upper trapezius

medial deltoid

posterior deltoid

rhomboids

triceps brachii

lower trapezius

latissimus dorsi

spinal erectors

internal oblique

gluteals

hamstrings

gastrocnemius

Index

A

abdominal crunch (stability ball exercise), 130

abdominal crunch (torso exercise), 113

abdominals, exercises for. *See also* medicine ball exercises; stability ball exercises
abdominal crunch, 113, 130
bicycles, 117
knee lifts, 107
oblique crunch, 114–15
single straight-arm pulldown, 93
straight-arm pulldown, 92

advanced shoulder stretch (standing stretch), 58

anterior deltoid, exercises for
dumbbell bench press, 90
opposite arm and leg raise, 108
paddle simulator, 98–99

arm circles (kneeling stretch), 36–37

axe chop (medicine ball exercise), 120

B

back extension (medicine ball exercise), 126

back extension (stability ball exercise), 136

back extension with twist (stability ball exercise), 137

back-paddling (paddling activity), 76

bar hang (standing stretch), 49

bent-over row (upper body exercise), 97

biceps brachii, exercises for
bent-over row, 97
lat pulldown, 94
one-arm row, 96
paddle simulator, 98–99
seated row, 95

bicycles (torso exercise), 117

boat pose (sitting stretch), 43

brachioradialis, exercises for
lat pulldown, 94
seated row, 95
upright row, 89

C

calf stretch with strap (lying stretch), 28

campground workout routine, 156–58

chest and shoulder stretch (standing stretch), 50

chest pass crunch (medicine ball exercise), 125

the chop (torso exercise), 109

conditioning programs, creating, 17. *See also* workout programs, types of
endurance training, 18–20
flexibility training, 18
strength training, 20–21

crocodile twist (lying stretch), 30–31

crossed arm stretch (kneeling stretch), 35

crossed knee lift (lying stretch), 25

crossover twist (lying stretch), 26

cross-training exercises (endurance training), 78–82

cycling (cross-training activity), 81

D

deep forward bend (Sun Salutation), 69

deltoids, exercises for
bent-over row, 97
dumbbell bench press, 90
lateral raise, 88
lat pulldown, 94
one-arm row, 96
opposite arm and leg raise, 108
paddle simulator, 98–99
seated row, 95
upright row, 89

downward-facing dog (kneeling stretch), 38

downward-facing dog (Sun Salutation), 67

drafting paddle (paddling activity), 75

drafting runs (cross-training activity), 81

dumbbell bench press (upper body exercise), 90

dumbbell pullover (upper body exercise), 91

E

elbow presses (lying stretch), 23

endurance training, 18–20, 72–73. *See also* workout programs, about

endurance training activities. *See also* workout programs, types of
cross-training, 78–82
paddling, 73–77

external obliques, exercises for
bicycles, 117
the chop, 109
lateral torso lift, 116
oblique crunch, 114–15
twisting lift, 110–11

external rotation I (upper body exercise), 86

external rotation II (upper body exercise), 87

F

flexibility training, 18, 22–23. *See also* workout programs, about

flexibility training exercises. *See also* Sun Salutation; workout programs, types of
lying stretches, 23–33
kneeling stretches, 34–41
sitting stretches, 42–48
standing stretches, 49–58

forward bend (Sun Salutation), 62
deep, 69

the frog (sitting stretch), 42

G

gastrocnemius, exercise for
split squat, 104

gluteals, exercises for
good morning exercise, 112
leg press, 100–101
opposite arm and leg raise, 108
split squat, 104
squat, 103
stiff leg deadlift, 106
walking lunge, 105

good morning exercise (torso exercise), 112

grasshopper pose (Sun Salutation), 65

gym workout program, 148–56

H

hamstrings, exercises for
good morning exercise, 112
leg press, 100–101
lying leg curl, 102
opposite arm and leg raise, 108
split squat, 104
squat, 103

hamstrings *(continued)*
   stiff leg deadlift, 106
   walking lunge, 105
hamstring stretch with
      strap (lying stretch),
      27
home workout program,
      140-48

I
iliotibial band stretch
      with strap (lying
      stretch), 31
injury prevention, flexi-
      bility training and,
      18, 22
internal obliques, exer-
      cises for
   bicycles, 117
   the chop, 109
   lateral torso lift, 116
   oblique crunch,
      114-15
   twisting lift, 110-11
interval paddling
      (paddling activity),
      74

K
Karvonen Method, for
      determining target
      heart rate, 19, 20
knee lifts (torso exer-
      cise), 107
kneeling stretches. *See*
      stretches, kneeling
kneeling with arms
      raised (stability ball
      exercise), 138

L
lactic acid, 83
land paddle with resist-
      ance bands (cross-
      training activity),
      78-79
lateral flexion (stability
      ball exercise), 135
lateral raise (upper body
      exercise), 88
lateral torso lift (torso
      exercise), 116
latissimus dorsi, exer-
      cises for
   bent-over row, 97
   the chop, 109
   dumbbell pullover,
      91
   lat pulldown, 94
   one-arm row, 96
   paddle simulator,
      98-99
   seated row, 95
   single straight-arm
      pulldown, 93
   straight-arm pull-
      down, 92
   twisting lift, 110-11
lat pulldown (upper
      body exercise), 94
leg press (lower body
      exercise), 100-101
lower body exercises
   leg press, 100-101
   lying leg curl, 102
   split squat, 104
   squat, 103
   stiff leg deadlift, 106
   walking lunge, 105

lower trapezius, exer-
      cise for
   opposite arm and leg
      raise, 108
lunge position (Sun
      Salutation), 63, 68
lying leg curl (lower
      body exercise),
      102
lying stretches. *See*
      stretches, lying

M
mad cat stretch (kneel-
      ing stretch), 34-35
medial deltoid, exercises
      for
   dumbbell bench
      press, 90
   lateral raise, 88
   opposite arm and leg
      raise, 108
medicine ball training,
      118-19
medicine ball exercises
   axe chop, 120
   back extension, 126
   chest pass crunch,
      125
   overhead toss, 123
   rotary torso toss, 124
   Russian twist, 122
   seated twist, 121
   standing torso rota-
      tion, 127
middle trapezius, exer-
      cises for
   bent-over row, 97
   lat pulldown, 94

one-arm row, 96
seated row, 95
modified hurdler stretch
(sitting stretch),
45
modified shoulder stand
(kneeling stretch),
39
mountain pose (Sun
Salutation), 61, 70
muscles. *See specific
muscles*

O

oblique crunch (torso
exercise), 114-15
obliques, exercises for
bicycles, 117
the chop, 109
lateral torso lift, 116
oblique crunch,
114-15
twisting lift, 110-11
one-arm row (upper
body exercise), 96
opposite arm and leg
raise (torso exer-
cise), 108
overhead toss (medicine
ball exercise), 123
overload principle,
72-73

P

paddle relays (paddling
activity), 76-77
paddle simulator (upper
body exercise),
98-99

paddling activities (en-
durance training),
73-77
paddling upstream (pad-
dling activity), 74
pain, responding to, 17,
22
partner towing (pad-
dling activity),
74-75
pectoralis major, exer-
cises for
dumbbell bench
press, 90
dumbbell pullover, 91
paddle simulator,
98-99
single straight-arm
pulldown, 93
straight-arm pull-
down, 92
pectoralis minor, exer-
cises for
dumbbell bench
press, 90
paddle simulator,
98-99
single straight-arm
pulldown, 93
straight-arm pull-
down, 92
the pike (stability ball
exercise), 134
plank position (Sun
Salutation), 64
poses. *See* flexibility
training exercises
poses, yoga. *See* Sun
Salutation

posterior deltoid, exer-
cises for
bent-over row, 97
lat pulldown, 94
one-arm row, 96
opposite arm and leg
raise, 108
paddle simulator,
98-99
seated row, 95
upright row, 89
prayer pose (Sun Saluta-
tion), 60, 71
psoas major, exercises
for
bicycles, 117
knee lifts, 107
pullovers (lying stretch),
24-25
push-up (stability ball
exercise), 133

Q

quadriceps, exercises
for
leg press, 100-101
split squat, 104
squat, 103
walking lunge, 105

R

rate of perceived exer-
tion (RPE), 19-20
resistance paddling
(paddling activity),
73-74
reverse triangle pose
(standing stretch),
55

rhomboids, exercises for
  bent-over row, 97
  lat pulldown, 94
  one-arm row, 96
  seated row, 95
rotary torso toss (medicine ball exercise), 124
rotator cuff, exercises for
  external rotation I, 86
  external rotation II, 87
rowing machines (cross-training activity), 79–80
Rs, five, of strength training, 84
running (cross-training activity), 81
Russian twist (medicine ball exercise), 122

S
seated lower-back stretch (sitting stretch), 48
seated row (upper body exercise), 95
seated torso twist (sitting stretch), 46
seated twist (medicine ball exercise), 121
serratus anterior, exercises for
  dumbbell pullover, 91
  single straight-arm pulldown, 93
  straight-arm pulldown, 92

shoulder pivots (kneeling stretch), 40
side lateral raise (kneeling stretch), 41
side reach (standing stretch), 54
simple twist (sitting stretch), 47
single straight-arm pulldown (upper body exercise), 93
sitting floor (sitting stretch), 44
sitting stretches. *See* stretches, sitting
spinal erectors, exercises for
  good morning exercise, 112
  opposite arm and leg raise, 108
split squat (lower body exercise), 104
squat (lower body exercise), 103
stability ball training, 128–29
stability ball exercises
  abdominal crunch, 130
  back extension, 136
  back extension with twist, 137
  kneeling with arms raised, 138
  lateral flexion, 135
  the pike, 134
  push-up, 133

trunk (torso) rotation, 132
  walk-out, 131
stair climbing (cross-training activity), 81
standing stretches. *See* stretches, standing
standing torso rotation (medicine ball exercise), 127
stiff leg deadlift (lower body exercise), 106
straight-arm pulldown (upper body exercise), 92
strength training, 20–21, 83–85, 118, 128–29. *See also* workout programs, about
strength training exercises. *See also* workout programs, types of
  lower body, 100–106
  torso, 107–17
  upper body, 86–99
stretches, kneeling
  arm circles, 36–37
  crossed arm stretch, 35
  downward-facing dog, 38
  mad cat stretch, 34–35
  modified shoulder stand, 39
  shoulder pivots, 40
  side lateral raise, 41

stretches, lying
  calf stretch with strap, 28
  crocodile twist, 30–31
  crossed knee lift, 25
  crossover twist, 26
  elbow presses, 23
  hamstring stretch with strap, 27
  iliotibial band stretch with strap, 31
  pullovers, 24–25
  superhero, 29
  upper spinal floor twist, 32–33
  upward-facing dog, 33
stretches, sitting
  boat pose, 43
  the frog, 42
  modified hurdler stretch, 45
  seated lower-back stretch, 48
  seated torso twist, 46
  simple twist, 47
  sitting floor, 44
stretches, standing
  advanced shoulder stretch, 58
  bar hang, 49
  chest and shoulder stretch, 50
  reverse triangle pose, 55
  side reach, 54
  triangle pose, 52–53
  wall sit, 56
  warrior pose, 51
  wrist stretch, 57

suicide drills (cross-training activity), 80
Sun Salutation, 59
  deep forward bend, 69
  downward-facing dog, 67
  forward bend, 62
  grasshopper pose, 65
  lunge position, 63, 68
  mountain pose, 61, 70
  plank position, 64
  prayer pose, 60, 71
  upward-facing dog, 66
superhero (lying stretch), 29
swimming (cross-training activity), 81–82

T
target exercise heart rate, 18–19
torso exercises. *See also* medicine ball exercises; stability ball exercises
  abdominal crunch, 113
  bicycles, 117
  the chop, 109
  good morning exercise, 112
  knee lifts, 107
  lateral torso lift, 116
  oblique crunch, 114–15
  opposite arm and leg raise, 108
  twisting lift, 110–11

trapezius, exercises for
  bent-over row, 97
  lat pulldown, 94
  one-arm row, 96
  opposite arm and leg raise, 108
  seated row, 95
  upright row, 89
triangle pose (standing stretch), 52–53
  reverse, 55
triceps brachii, exercises for
  dumbbell bench press, 90
  dumbbell pullover, 91
  paddle simulator, 98–99
  single straight-arm pulldown, 93
  straight-arm pulldown, 92
trunk (torso) rotation (stability ball exercise), 132
tug-of-war (paddling activity), 75, 76
twisting lift (torso exercise), 110–11

U
underwater swimming (cross-training activity), 82
upper body exercises. *See also* stability ball exercises
  bent-over row, 97

upper body exercises
(continued)
dumbbell bench
press, 90
dumbbell pullover, 91
external rotation I, 86
external rotation II, 87
lateral raise, 88
lat pulldown, 94
one-arm row, 96
paddle simulator,
98–99
seated row, 95
single straight-arm
pulldown, 93
straight-arm pull-
down, 92
upright row, 89
upper spinal floor twist
(lying stretch),
32–33

upper trapezius, exer-
cise for
upright row, 89
upright row (upper
body exercise), 89
upward-facing dog (ly-
ing stretch), 33
upward-facing dog (Sun
Salutation), 66

W
walking (cross-training
activity), 81
walking lunge (lower
body exercise), 105
walk-out (stability ball
exercise), 131
wall sit (standing
stretch), 56
warrior pose (standing
stretch), 51

water sprints (cross-
training activity), 80
workout programs,
about, 21, 139–40
workout programs,
types of
gym, 148–56
home, 140–48
overnight camp-
ground routine,
156–58
wrist stretch (standing
stretch), 57

Y
yoga warm-up poses.
See Sun Salutation